THE ALCHEMY OF PEACE

Transforming Your Life Through the Principles of Magical Ho'oponopono

GANDHIMATHI M

Made with ♥ on the Notion Press Platform
www.notionpress.com

The Alchemy of Peace

Transforming Your Life Through the Principles of Magical Ho'oponopono

The Alchemy of Peace is a compelling book focused on Magical Ho'oponopono. It suggests a transformative process where inner peace is crafted through a form of spiritual or emotional transformation, much like how alchemy turns base materials into gold. This aligns well with the themes of personal growth, healing, and the continuous journey that Ho'oponopono represents.

If you want to convey the idea that peace is achieved through a transformative and almost magical process, *The Alchemy of Peace* is a fitting choice. It adds a sense of depth and magic to the practice, emphasising its profound impact on the practitioner's life.

What You'll Discover:

1. **The Essence of Magical Ho'oponopono:** Uncover the fundamental principles of Ho'oponopono and how this practice serves as a powerful tool for personal and emotional alchemy. Learn about its origins and the transformative potential it holds for healing and inner peace.

2. **Transformative Practices:** Explore step-by-step practices that turn emotional challenges into opportunities for growth. Understand how simple yet profound actions, such as forgiveness, gratitude, and self-love, can lead to significant inner transformation.

3. **Alchemy of Self-Discovery:** Dive into exercises and reflections designed to help you discover your true self. Learn how to apply Ho'oponopono to release past grievances and embrace a deeper sense of who you are, allowing your authentic self to shine through.

4. **Healing Through Inner Alchemy:** Discover how the principles of Ho'oponopono can heal emotional wounds and foster inner peace. Explore practical techniques to address unresolved issues and transform negative patterns into positive change.

5. **Cultivating Lasting Peace:** Learn how to integrate Ho'oponopono into your daily life to maintain a state of peace and balance. Find out how to create

a sustainable practice that adapts to your evolving needs and enhances your overall well-being.

6. **The Journey of Transformation:** Embrace the idea that achieving inner peace is a continuous journey of personal transformation. Understand how Ho'oponopono guides you through this process, helping you navigate life's challenges with grace and resilience.

Why This Book Is for You:

The Alchemy of Peace is crafted for anyone seeking to transform their inner world and achieve lasting peace. Whether you're new to Ho'oponopono or looking to deepen your practice, this book provides insightful guidance and practical tools to help you harness the magical power of personal alchemy.

Begin Your Journey:

Embark on a journey of self-discovery and transformation with *The Alchemy of Peace.* Discover how the practice of Ho'oponopono can turn the base elements of your emotional experiences into the gold of inner peace and fulfilment.

Contents

Foreword

In a world often filled with noise, conflict, and the relentless pace of daily life, the search for inner peace becomes not just a desire but a necessity. *The Alchemy of Peace* offers a gentle, yet profound, invitation to embark on this journey of self-discovery and transformation through the principles of Ho'oponopono. Much like the ancient art of alchemy—where base metals are transformed into gold—this book reveals how we can transmute our emotional burdens into the gold of forgiveness, healing, and peace.

Drawing from the rich tradition of Hawaiian wisdom, *The Alchemy of Peace* serves as a guide to a practice that is both beautifully simple and infinitely deep. The core phrases of Ho'oponopono—"I'm sorry," "Please forgive me," "Thank you," and "I love you"—may seem modest, yet within them lies a power that can unlock deep healing and reconciliation. Through the insights and practical exercises woven throughout these pages, readers will discover how these words can be tools for clearing emotional clutter, restoring relationships, and cultivating a profound sense of inner balance.

This book doesn't just explain Ho'oponopono; it invites you to experience it. It provides practices, reflections, and stories that illustrate the transformative potential of this ancient art. You are encouraged not just to read, but to participate—to say the words, feel their impact, and witness the shifts that follow.

As you turn these pages, let your heart remain open to the possibility of change. Whether you are seeking to heal past wounds, improve relationships, or simply find a deeper sense of calm, *The Alchemy of Peace* offers a roadmap toward a more harmonious, resilient, and loving life. May this book inspire you, as it has inspired me, to embrace the magic of personal alchemy and uncover the peace that lies within.

– Reika Hue

– My Mentor, Friend, and Colleague

Dedication

To my beloved brother, **Saravanan M**, You were not just my sibling but the pillar of my strength, the unwavering beacon of hope in my darkest times, and the wind beneath my wings during my triumphs.

Your love, wisdom, and endless support uplifted my life in ways words can never fully capture. You believed in me when I doubted myself and stood by me with unshakeable faith. Every step I take and every success I achieve carries your indelible mark.

Though you are no longer here in person, your presence lives on in every heartbeat, every thought, and every word of this book. This work is a tribute to your legacy, reflecting the peace, resilience, and love you inspired in me.

Acknowledgement

First and foremost, I extend my deepest gratitude to my mom and dad, whose love, guidance, and sacrifices have shaped me into the person I am today. Your unwavering support has made everything possible.

To my dear siblings—my brother, M. Saravanan, my brother, B. Santhosh, and my sister, S. Indira, thank you for your constant encouragement and unwavering belief in my abilities. Your support has been a cornerstone of my journey.

I'm truly grateful to my husband, A. Sugumar, for his constant support and belief in me. He has been my anchor throughout this journey. Thank you for being my rock and helping me bring this book to life.

I am eternally grateful to my son, S. Arishraj, whose endless support has been a great source of joy and motivation. To my loving daughters, S. Sakthi and S. Nirupama, you have been a constant source of inspiration and happiness. You remind me daily of the importance of love and purpose in life.

My sincere thanks go to my esteemed coach, Dr. Manjunath. Your expertise and motivation have played a pivotal role in my personal and professional growth. Your guidance has driven me to bring this book to life.

I also wish to extend special thanks to my friend and mentor, J. Sakthivel. Your friendship, encouragement, and unwavering support have been a constant source of strength throughout this journey. Thank you for always being there for me.

Lastly, I am immensely thankful to my community of friends— G. Ramadevi, S. Vijayalakshmi, Dr. Annie Freeda, P. Pandian, RC. Rajesh, Thanuja Jayaram, Dr. Shilpa, Bhargav Kommu, Rajlaxmi, Nirmala, and Saurav Das. Your belief in me and your continuous support have been truly inspiring. I am fortunate to have walked this path with you by my side.

To all of you, thank you for your unwavering support in helping me complete this book. It stands as a testament to your belief in me, and for that, I am forever grateful.

About the Author

Gandhimathi M is a dynamic professional and a world record holder in Yoga, driven by her passion for Yoga and Meditation. Her journey has been marked by an unwavering commitment to personal well-being and inspiring others around her. As an accomplished Ho'oponopono practitioner and a Magical Healer, Gandhimathi has found peace and transformation through this ancient Hawaiian practice, which motivated her to write this book to share its powerful impact on her life.

Her love for learning extends to reading, where she holds a speed-reading award of 1500 words per minute. Known for her impactful communication, she has also earned the 'Most Impactful Speaker' award. A proud recipient of the 'Pro Award' from Dr. Manjunath's

Diamond community, Gandhimathi stands as a symbol of dedication and achievement.

Outside her professional life, she is a lovable person who enjoys spending quality time with her family and friends. Music is one of her greatest joys, both in singing and listening. Her athletic skills, recognised during her school and college years, continue to reflect her active lifestyle. Gandhimathi's holistic approach to life, through yoga, meditation, Ho'oponopono, and mastering NLP, makes her a guiding light to all who know her.

Introduction:
What is Ho'oponopono?

In a world where challenges and conflicts are part of everyday life, finding inner peace and harmonious relationships can often feel out of reach. However, the ancient Hawaiian practice of Ho'oponopono offers a time-tested way to address these universal struggles and find healing and reconciliation. Ho'oponopono is based on the idea that true peace starts from within. It provides a clear method for fixing the broken pieces in our lives and improving our relationships.

At its essence, Ho'oponopono is about bringing balance and harmony into our lives. The term "Ho'oponopono" means "to make right" or "to correct," which reflects its goal of addressing and mending the conflicts we have with ourselves and others. This practice emphasises personal responsibility for our actions, thoughts, and their effects. By adopting a mindset of accountability and forgiveness, we can change how we handle conflicts and challenges.

Central to Ho'oponopono are four simple but powerful phrases: "I'm sorry," "Please forgive me," "Thank you," and "I love you." These phrases are more than just words; they are genuine expressions of regret, requests for forgiveness, gratitude, and unconditional love. Incorporating these phrases into our daily lives helps us start a process of meaningful healing and transformation.

This book is an invitation to explore the depths of Ho'oponopono and see how its principles can bring clarity and peace to your life. We will dive into the concepts and practices of Ho'oponopono, sharing practical applications and inspiring stories that highlight its transformative power. The goal is to help you understand and use these principles so you can experience their benefits directly.

From my own experience, I can attest to the deep effect that Ho'oponopono has had on my life. Applying these principles has led to significant positive changes in both my personal and professional life. I have found greater success and peace, and I'm excited to share these insights with you. Through Ho'oponopono, I have learned to navigate life's challenges more smoothly and build stronger, more harmonious relationships.

As you begin this journey, I encourage you to approach it with an open heart and mind. The wisdom of Ho'oponopono offers a path to healing past wounds and developing a mindset of love and kindness. This shift in perspective can lead to deep personal growth and a more fulfilling life. By letting go of past grievances and embracing forgiveness, you can discover a deeper sense of joy and satisfaction.

I hope my experiences with Ho'oponopono inspire you to explore these practices and incorporate them into your life. This book is not just a guide to understanding Ho'oponopono; it is an invitation to experience its transformative power and make it a key part of your journey toward a more balanced and harmonious life.

Chapter 1

The Power of Apology 'Saying Sorry'

"An apology is the superglue of life. It can repair just about anything."

– Lynn Johnston

Saying sorry is the first step in the practice of Ho'oponopono, where we begin the journey of healing by acknowledging our role in conflicts and taking responsibility for our actions. This chapter explores how genuinely saying sorry can lead to meaningful personal and relational transformation.

Understanding Responsibility

Taking responsibility means recognising how our actions, words, and even thoughts contribute to disharmony. It's not about self-blame but about understanding the influence we have on situations. This awareness is the key to healing and growth.

Self-Reflection: Think about past situations where your actions may have caused hurt. Reflect on how acknowledging this can shift your perspective and open the path to healing.

Example: Imagine a time when a harsh comment led to a disagreement with a friend. By reflecting on this and saying sorry, you not only acknowledge the hurt caused but also take the first step towards healing the relationship.

Empathy: Develop empathy by trying to see situations from others' points of view. Understanding the impact of your actions from their perspective fosters deeper connections and healing.

Example: Consider a scenario where you missed an important event for a loved one. By seeing the situation from their viewpoint, you can understand their feelings of disappointment. Saying sorry becomes a way to bridge the gap and restore harmony.

Genuine Apology

A genuine apology goes beyond just saying sorry. It is an expression of our willingness to make amends, heal wounds, and rebuild trust. When we apologise with true intent, we not only fix the immediate hurt but also strengthen our relationships by showing that we value the other person's feelings and our connection with them. Let's break down what makes an apology sincere and effective.

1. Components of a Sincere Apology:

a) Acknowledgement:

The first step in a genuine apology is to clearly state what you are sorry for. It involves identifying the specific action or behaviour that caused harm and verbalising it. For example, if you unintentionally hurt a friend's feelings by cancelling plans last minute, you might say, "I'm sorry for cancelling our plans at the last minute and making you feel unimportant." This acknowledgement shows that you are aware of your actions and their impact.

b) Expression of Regret:

Along with acknowledgement, expressing genuine regret is crucial. This isn't just about saying the words but about conveying that you truly feel sorrowful for the hurt caused. For instance, you might add, "I regret that my actions made you feel overlooked, and I wish I had handled the situation differently." This step helps to communicate that you care about the other person's feelings and that their well-being matters to you.

c) Commitment to Change:

A genuine apology also involves a commitment to change. This means expressing your intention to avoid repeating the behaviour that caused harm. Continuing the previous example, you might say, "In the future, I will make sure to communicate better and prioritise our plans." This commitment reassures the other person that you are taking steps to prevent similar issues from arising.

d) Request for Forgiveness:

Finally, a heartfelt apology often includes a humble request for forgiveness, without assuming that it will automatically be granted. You might say, "I hope you can forgive me, but I understand if you need time." This request acknowledges the other person's right to feel hurt and their need for time to heal.

Example Scenarios:

Imagine you had a misunderstanding with a colleague that led to an argument. After cooling off, you reflect on your part in the conflict and decide to apologise. A sincere apology might look like this:

- **Acknowledgement:** "I'm sorry for not listening to your ideas during the meeting."
- **Expression of Regret:** "I regret dismissing your input. It wasn't fair to you, and I realise it might have made you feel undervalued."
- **Commitment to Change:** "In the future, I will make a conscious effort to consider everyone's perspectives."
- **Request for Forgiveness:** "I hope you can forgive me, and I'm open to any feedback on how I can improve."

Similarly, imagine you had an argument with a family member where you said something hurtful in the heat of the moment. Reflecting on this later, you realise the impact of your words.

- **Acknowledgement:** "I'm sorry for what I said earlier."
- **Expression of Regret:** "It was wrong, and I regret causing you pain."
- **Commitment to Change:** "I want to work on controlling my temper and being more thoughtful in our conversations,"
- **Request for Forgiveness:** "I hope you can forgive me when you're ready."

By following these steps, you demonstrate that your apology is thoughtful, sincere, and rooted in a desire to maintain and strengthen the relationship.

Real life example of Apology:.

One day, my sister and I faced some complaints that had left us feeling quite troubled. We were informed that our actions had caused significant difficulties, including a tough journey home under the hot sun and facing consequences for our mistakes. This feedback made us realise how much we had struggled because of it. When my mom heard about everything, she felt a deep sense of sympathy for us. She understood that her own thoughts and expectations might have played a role in our difficulties. She felt truly 'sorry' for the hardship we had experienced and the way we were punished.

In a heartfelt moment, she came to us and expressed her regret. She told us that because of her thoughts, we had suffered more than we should have. She apologised and asked us to let go of any worry or guilt we might still be holding onto. Her words were meant to release us from the burden of the past.

From that point on, things started to improve. We let go of the worry and guilt that had been weighing us down. My mom's compassion and understanding brought us relief, and we were able to move forward with a lighter heart. Her actions and words had turned the situation around, and we felt a renewed sense of peace.

Practical Exercises

Incorporating the practice of saying sorry and taking responsibility into your daily life can lead to profound personal and relational growth. These exercises are designed to help you internalise these principles and make them a natural part of how you interact with the world.

1. Reflective Journaling

Reflective journaling is a powerful tool for self-awareness and personal growth. It allows you to explore your actions, thoughts, and their impact on others.

a. **Daily Reflection**: At the end of each day, take a moment to reflect on your interactions. Think about any moments where you might have acted or spoken in a way that caused hurt or misunderstanding. Write about these situations, focusing on what happened, how you felt, and the impact of your actions on others.

b. **Learning from the Past**: Reflect on past situations where you wish you had acted differently. By revisiting these moments, you can gain insights into your patterns of behaviour. Write down what you could have done differently and how you might handle similar situations in the future. This exercise helps you to learn from your mistakes and prevents you from repeating them.

c. **Embracing Responsibility**: Use your journal to explore how taking responsibility for your actions feels. Write about how acknowledging your mistakes and saying sorry has affected your relationships and your own sense of self.

Example: After an argument with a friend, you might reflect in your journal about what triggered your response, how your words may have hurt them, and what you could have done to approach the situation differently.

2. Daily Affirmations

Affirmations are positive statements that can help you cultivate a mindset of responsibility and openness to learning from your mistakes. They work by reinforcing positive beliefs and behaviours.

a. **Creating Affirmations**: Develop a set of affirmations that resonate with your journey of saying sorry and taking responsibility. These might include statements like, "I am open to recognising my mistakes and learning from them," or "I take responsibility for my actions and their impact on others."

b. **Morning Routine**: Incorporate these affirmations into your morning routine. Start your day by repeating them to yourself, either silently or out loud. This practice helps set a positive tone for the day and keeps you mindful of your commitment to personal growth.

c. **Reflecting on Progress**: As you use these affirmations daily, take time to reflect on how they influence your behaviour and mindset. Do you find it easier to acknowledge mistakes and say sorry? Are you more aware of your actions and their impact on others?

Example: You might start your day with the affirmation, **"I am committed to understanding the effects of my words and actions."**.

3. Role-Playing

Role-playing is a practical and interactive way to practice apologising in a safe and controlled environment. It allows you to explore different scenarios and refine your approach to saying sorry.

a. **Setting Up Scenarios**: Choose scenarios that reflect real-life situations where you might need to apologise. This could be a disagreement with a friend, a misunderstanding at work, or a situation where your actions caused unintended harm.

b. **Practising Sincerity**: During the role-play, focus on being sincere. Acknowledge the specific action you are sorry for, express genuine regret, and communicate your intention to make things right. Practising this helps you become more comfortable with the process and ensures your apologies are heartfelt.

c. **Understanding Emotions**: Pay attention to the emotions involved in the apology—both yours and the other person's. Role-playing allows you to explore these emotions in a controlled setting, helping you to develop empathy and a deeper understanding of the impact of your actions.

Example: In a role-playing exercise, you might practice apologising to a colleague for interrupting them during a meeting. Through this practice, you can explore how to express your regret genuinely and how to convey your commitment to being more mindful in the future.

Genuine Apology is a powerful step toward healing, allowing us to clear emotional and relational blockages. By embracing this practice, we lay the foundation for forgiveness and deeper connections with ourselves and others.

Points to Remember

- **Apology Heals Relationships:** Saying sorry can fix and improve your relationships.
- **Take Responsibility:** Admitting your mistakes helps you grow and repair any harm done.
- **Use Empathy:** Understand how the other person feels to make your apology more sincere.
- **Apology Steps:** Say what you did wrong, show regret, promise to improve, and ask for forgiveness.
- **Apology Brings Peace:** A sincere apology makes your relationships stronger and brings peace.

Chapter 2

Welcoming Forgiveness

"In the process of letting go you will lose many things from the past, but you will find yourself."

– Deepak Chopra

Forgiveness is a powerful and transformative force that can liberate us from mental and emotional pain, ultimately leading to greater happiness. Forgiveness involves the decision to release anger and hatred. Although the hurt from a past event might still be present, choosing to forgive can lessen its impact on our lives. This process helps in diminishing the grip that negative experiences have on our mental and emotional state. By forgiving, we free ourselves from being controlled by past grievances, enabling us to experience more peace and happiness in our lives.

Letting Go

Holding onto complaints and negative feelings affects us more deeply than it does the person or situation we are angry with. Often, we don't realise how much of our energy is consumed by these lingering negative emotions. When we hold onto anger and resentment, we are investing significant effort and energy into maintaining these feelings. This can drain our emotional resources and prevent us from experiencing joy and satisfaction.

Many people carry their anger for so long that they become accustomed to it. They may not even notice the extent to which it influences their lives. This persistent negativity can cloud our judgement, affect our relationships, and impact our overall quality of life. By letting go of these feelings, we begin to release the hold that anger and resentment have over us. This can lead to a profound sense of relief and freedom, allowing us to approach life with a renewed sense of energy and positivity.

Forgiveness is not always easy, but it is a crucial step towards personal healing and emotional well-being. It requires courage to confront and release the hurt that we carry. However, the rewards of forgiveness—inner peace, reduced stress, and improved relationships—are well worth the effort. By embracing forgiveness, we take a significant step towards reclaiming our happiness and living a more fulfilling life.

To Ease Negative Feelings: The Simple Practice of Forgiveness Meditation

Forgiveness meditation is a straightforward yet powerful practice designed to help us release negative emotions and maintain a positive outlook. Given that we're all human, it's natural to encounter situations that upset us or cause emotional pain. This practice serves as a valuable tool for managing these feelings and keeping our energy positive and resilient.

1. **The Burden of Anger:** When we hold onto anger, it doesn't just affect our emotional state—it can also have tangible effects on our physical well-being. Anger and resentment are heavy burdens that can weigh us down mentally and physically. For example:

2. **Mental Impact:** Constant anger can lead to stress, anxiety, and even depression. Imagine a situation where someone has wronged you, and you constantly chew over the event, replaying it in your mind. This persistent focus on anger keeps you in a state of emotional turmoil, making it difficult to concentrate on other aspects of your life. Over time, this can drain your mental health and diminish your overall sense of well-being.

3. **Physical Impact:** The stress from holding onto anger can manifest in physical symptoms. Research shows that chronic anger and stress can lead to issues such as headaches, high blood pressure, and even heart disease. For instance, if you find yourself frequently tense and agitated because of unresolved anger, you might experience tension headaches or a racing heart, reflecting the strain this emotion places on your body.

4. **Deciding to Let Go:** Forgiveness is a deliberate choice to release the hold that anger and resentment have on us. It's about deciding to move forward and seek peace rather than remaining stuck in negativity. Here are some examples of how making this choice can transform your experience:

a. **Family Example:** Imagine a situation where a family member, say your sibling, forgets to attend an important family event you organized, such as a birthday celebration for a loved one. Their absence is particularly hurtful because they had promised to be there, and their presence was important to you.

You might initially feel a mix of emotions—hurt, frustration, and even anger. It's natural to replay the scenario in your mind, thinking about how inconsiderate they were and how their absence affected the event. This focus on their mistake can lead to lasting negative feelings and tension in your relationship.

Instead of letting these feelings worsen, you decide to practice forgiveness. Here's how you might approach this:

a) **Acknowledge Your Feelings:** Start by recognising and accepting your emotions. You might say to yourself, "I feel hurt and angry because my sibling didn't show up. Their absence made me feel unimportant."

b) **Reflect on the Situation:** Consider why your sibling might have missed the event. They could have had an emergency or unforeseen issue. Understanding their perspective can help you feel more compassionate.

c) **Choose to Let Go:** Actively decide to release the anger and hurt. This doesn't mean you ignore your feelings, but rather you choose not to let them control you. You might think, "I choose to let go of this anger. Holding onto it only harms our relationship and my own peace of mind."

d) **Communicate and Rebuild:** If appropriate, have a calm conversation with your sibling about how their absence affected you. Express your feelings without blaming them. For example, you might say, "I missed you at the family event and felt disappointed. I understand things come up, but I wanted to share how it impacted me."

By practising forgiveness in this way, you can move past the hurt and focus on maintaining a positive relationship with your sibling. This approach helps you to heal emotionally and strengthens your family bonds, allowing for a more harmonious and supportive relationship.

b. **Professional Example**: Imagine you've put in extensive effort on a key project at work. You've stayed late, managed complex tasks, and contributed valuable ideas. When the project is presented, you find that a colleague is taking credit for much of the work you did. Initially, this causes a wave of anger, frustration, and disappointment. You feel that your hard work is being overshadowed, and this injustice makes it difficult to concentrate and collaborate effectively.

Here's how practising forgiveness can help in this professional scenario:

a) **Acknowledge Your Emotions:** Recognise and accept how you feel. For instance, you might acknowledge, "I'm feeling very angry and frustrated because my colleague is taking credit for my work. This feels unfair and disrespectful."

b) **Reflect on the Situation:** Consider possible reasons behind your colleague's actions. They might be under pressure, seeking recognition, or simply making a mistake. While this doesn't excuse their behaviour, understanding their possible motivations can help you approach the situation with more empathy.

c) **Choose to Let Go:** Decide to release the negative feelings you're holding onto. This doesn't mean you approve of what happened, but rather that you choose not to let this situation consume your energy. You might think, "I choose to let go of this anger. Holding onto it will only affect my own work performance and well-being."

d) **Focus on Productive Action:** Redirect your energy toward positive actions. You could document your contributions to ensure your efforts are recognised in the future. For example, you might keep detailed records of your work or seek regular feedback to maintain visibility.

e) **Maintain Professionalism:** Engage with your colleague professionally, without letting the situation impact your interactions. If appropriate, have a constructive conversation with them about the project and your contributions. You might say, "I wanted to clarify my role in the project. I worked on X, Y, and Z, and I think it's important for us to recognise everyone's contributions accurately."

f) **Embrace a Positive Work Environment:** Forgiving your colleague helps you maintain a positive work atmosphere. By not letting anger cloud your judgement, you contribute to a more collaborative and supportive team environment. It reduces the stress you carry, allowing you to focus on your work and personal growth.

By practising forgiveness in this professional setting, you can overcome the initial anger and frustration, approach the situation with a clearer mind, and continue to work productively. Forgiveness allows you to let go of the negative emotions and move forward in a constructive manner, benefiting both your personal well-being and the overall work environment.

c. **Transformative Power:** Forgiveness has the power to transform our lives, allowing us to experience emotional freedom and healing.

A. **Self-Forgiveness:** Start by forgiving yourself for past mistakes, recognising that self-care is essential for growth.

B. **Forgiving Others:** Understand that forgiving others does not ignore their actions, but frees you from their hold.

Real life example of forgiveness: Once I was completely down when I lost my beloved brother and was doubtful about how to move things forward. Suddenly, I met a friend, Megala, and we were part of a Prana Healing community. She connected with me to suggest ways to overcome the barriers in my life. She explained how she and her family struggled with their past karma and black magic, which caused both her son and daughter to not succeed in their personal lives, leading them into deep depression. So, they started practising a daily ritual of asking forgiveness from all those people who suffered because of their behaviours and actions, using the phrase "Please forgive me" while remembering the faces of those they knew and recalling the souls of those they did not. They also started forgiving all those who had made them suffer as well.

After everyday practice of heartfelt forgiveness to self and to all known and unknown people, slowly the entire family was able to rise from the downtrodden and lead to positivity and gained strong energy. Today, both her son and daughter were blessed with two kids each and leading a peaceful and happiest life with their families.

Lesson learned here is, If you wanted to be forgiven, firstly you would need to forgive others for their mistakes and let go of the anger and hatred. Thus, you'll be able to gain energy, inner peace, and happiness forever. Thus,

I was able to learn and follow the forgiveness meditation, slowly started letting go of all the pain and gained a lot of energy. Thus, things started falling into the right place and continuing the journey of forgiveness in all aspects. By following the practical exercises, you'll be able to learn and apply forgiveness in your everyday life, which would help you to overcome similar barriers in your own journey.

Practical Exercises for Cultivating Forgiveness

Engaging in practical exercises can significantly aid in the practice of forgiveness. These exercises help you process your emotions, release resentment, and cultivate a more forgiving mindset. Here are detailed descriptions and steps for each exercise:

1. Guided Meditations

Guided meditations for forgiveness are structured practices that help you focus on letting go of negative emotions and nurturing a kind mindset. These meditations often involve visualisation techniques and soothing guidance to help you release anger, hatred, and open your heart to forgiveness.

Steps:

a. **Find a Quiet Space:** Choose a calm and comfortable place where you won't be disturbed. Sit or lie down in a relaxed position.

b. **Meditation:**

   i) Take three deep breaths; focus on your breath while you inhale and exhale.

   ii) Now, bring your attention to your thoughts as they come and go. Look at each thought as a passing event. Think of your mind as the sky and your thoughts as the passing clouds. Simply be aware of them – don't become or judge them.

   iii) Bring your attention back to your breathing. As you exhale, let go of all the negative emotions and as you inhale, bring kindness and care to yourself

   iv) Now, bring to mind what you have to forgive. If it was a mistake from your past or someone who has hurt you. First visualise your face and from the bottom of your heart simply say "I forgive myself". Next, for others, similarly from the very bottom of the heart, say their name(s) or bring their face(s) and then say "I forgive you". For example, you might say to yourself, "I am here to release my anger and open my heart to forgiveness."

v) Now slowly inhale and exhale three times, then rub your palm and place it on your face. Open your eyes with a big smile as you look into your palm. Meditation ends.

c. **Embrace the Experience:** Allow yourself to fully immerse in the meditation. Pay attention to any emotions that arise and gently guide your focus back to the practice.

d. **Reflect:** After the meditation, take a few moments to reflect on the experience. Notice any shifts in your feelings or perspective regarding the person or situation you were focusing on.

Example: During a guided forgiveness meditation, you might visualisc a person who has hurt you and then imagine sending them positive energy and wishing them well. This visualisation helps you release the negative feelings associated with them.

2. Writing Letters of Forgiveness

Writing letters of forgiveness is a therapeutic exercise that allows you to articulate your feelings and thoughts towards someone you need to forgive. These letters are often written without the intention of sending them, serving as a tool for emotional processing and closure.

Steps:

a. **Choose Your Subject:** Identify the person or situation you need to forgive. This could be someone who has hurt you or a past event that still affects you.

b. **Write the Letter:** Begin writing a letter addressing the person or situation. Start with a clear statement of what you are forgiving and why. Be honest about your feelings and experiences.

c. **Express Your Emotions:** Detail how the situation has affected you and any pain or anger you've been holding onto. Include expressions of how you wish to move forward.

d. **Offer Forgiveness:** Clearly state your intention to forgive. You might write something like, "I am choosing to forgive you for the hurt you caused me. I want to let go of this pain and move forward with my life."

e. **Seek Closure:** Conclude the letter with a sense of closure. You don't need to send the letter; instead, consider it as a way to process and release your emotions.

f. **Reflect:** After writing the letter, reflect on how the process has affected you. Notice any changes in your feelings towards the person or situation.

Example: You might write a letter to a former friend who let down your trust. In the letter, you acknowledge the hurt, express how it impacted you, and ultimately offer forgiveness to release the burden of resentment.

3. Forgiveness Journaling

Forgiveness journaling involves regularly reflecting on people or situations where forgiveness is needed. This exercise helps you process your feelings, track your progress, and gain insight into your emotional journey.

Steps:

a. **Set Up Your Journal:** Use a notebook or digital journal dedicated to your forgiveness practice. Begin with a date and a brief description of the situation or person you are focusing on.

b. **Reflect on the Situation:** Write about the person or event you need to forgive. Describe the details of what happened, how it made you feel, and any ongoing impact it has on your life.

c. **Explore Your Emotions:** Explore your feelings of hurt, anger, or resentment. Be honest about your emotions and how they affect you.

d. **Consider Forgiveness:** Reflect on the process of forgiveness. What might it look like to forgive this person or situation? How would letting go of these feelings benefit you?

e. **Track Your Progress:** Regularly revisit your journal entries to see how your feelings evolve over time. Note any changes in your perspective or emotional state.

f. **Set Forgiveness Goals:** Use your journal to set goals for your forgiveness journey. For example, you might write, "My goal this week is to work on letting go of anger towards my colleague."

Example: You might journal about a recurring conflict with a family member. Through this practice, you explore your feelings, understand your desire for forgiveness, and notice how your perspective changes as you work through your emotions. By engaging in these practical exercises, you create a space for healing and transformation. Each exercise helps you process and release negative emotions, ultimately leading to a more forgiving and peaceful mindset.

Although it's tough to forgive people and what they did, it's even tougher to stay mad or upset because that hurts us more. It's beneficial for everyone to let go and move forward. Holding onto negative emotions only harms us and brings suffering, keeping us from living a fulfilling and loving life. Forgiving is a gift you give to yourself. By letting go of anger and hatred, you create space for healing and joy. Forgiveness is an ongoing journey, and each step brings you closer to inner peace. Remember, forgiveness is not just about the other person; it's a gift you give to yourself to enhance your own well-being and happiness.

Points to remember

- **Release for Inner Peace**: Letting go of anger and hatred frees you from emotional pain and opens the door to happiness.
- **Forgiveness Is a Choice**: Forgiveness isn't about forgetting the wrongs done to you; it's a conscious decision to move forward and heal.
- **The Burden of Anger**: Holding onto anger affects both your mental and physical well-being. Letting go can bring relief and better health.
- **Practical Steps**: Engage in forgiveness practices like meditation, writing letters, or journaling to help process emotions and embrace forgiveness.
- **Transformative Power**: Forgiveness transforms your life by freeing you from the past, allowing for emotional healing and a more fulfilling future.

Chapter 3

The Gratitude Connection

"The more we express our gratitude to others, the more we discover our own happiness."

– Walt Whitman

Gratitude turns what little you have into abundance. Gratitude is so much more than saying thank you.

Gratitude is a powerful practice that shifts our focus from what we lack to what we have, nurturing positivity and well-being. This chapter delves into how gratitude enhances our lives and strengthens our connections with others.

In our fast-paced, rushed world, taking the time to slow down allows our minds to follow suit. Even when reflecting on the day's events, thinking through a problem, or simply daydreaming, I've learned to take a moment to be thankful. One effective way to practice gratitude is by writing down what we are thankful for. Practising gratitude is a powerful, healthy, and easy way to improve our emotional state.

Impact on Health

Gratitude has significant benefits for mental and physical health, promoting happiness and reducing stress. It's a powerful practice that can profoundly impact our mental and physical well-being. Embracing gratitude can transform our outlook on life, leading to significant improvements in our health and happiness. Here's a detailed exploration of how gratitude benefits us psychologically and physically, supported by personal experiences and broader insights.

1. ***Psychological Benefits:*** Improves mood, reduces depression, and enhances overall life satisfaction.

   a) **Improves Mood**: Gratitude acts as a natural mood enhancer. When we regularly acknowledge and appreciate the positive aspects of our lives, it fosters a sense of pleasure and joy. For example, when I began incorporating gratitude into my daily routine, I noticed a significant shift in my mood. I felt more optimistic and less bogged down by daily stresses. This positive shift not only improved my overall outlook but also enhanced my interactions with others.

b) **Reduces Depression**: Numerous studies have shown that gratitude can play a crucial role in alleviating symptoms of depression. By focusing on what we have rather than what we lack, we break the cycle of negative thinking that often fuels depression. In my own life, practising gratitude helped me to shift my focus away from persistent worries and towards a more positive perspective. This shift contributed to a decrease in feelings of hopelessness and a greater sense of well-being.

c) **Enhances Overall Life Satisfaction**: Regular expressions of gratitude have been linked to increased satisfaction with life. By appreciating the small and big things, we start to see the beauty in everyday moments. Personally, I've found that keeping a gratitude journal—where I note things I'm thankful for each day—has led to a deeper appreciation of my life. This practice has enriched my writing by helping me stay grounded and appreciative of life's simple joys.

2. ***Physical Benefits***: Linked to better sleep, lower blood pressure, and a stronger immune system.

a) **Better Sleep**: Gratitude is associated with improved sleep quality. I've found that writing down things

I'm grateful for before going to sleep has helped me fall asleep more easily and wake up feeling refreshed.

b) **Lower Blood Pressure**: Regular gratitude practices can contribute to lower blood pressure. The act of feeling thankful and expressing appreciation can lead to relaxation and reduced stress levels. Personally, when practising gratitude, I've experienced a sense of calm, relaxation, and help to maintain healthy blood pressure levels.

c) **Stronger Immune System**: Gratitude can strengthen the immune system, making us less susceptible to illnesses. Although it might seem indirect, the stress-reducing effects of gratitude help support overall health. In my experience, feeling grateful has improved my resilience to stress-related ailments, contributing to a stronger immune system.

Cultivating Gratitude

Cultivating a mindset of gratitude involves consciously recognising and appreciating the positive aspects of life, even amidst challenges. This practice can significantly enhance your overall well-being and lead to a more fulfilling and balanced life. Here's a detailed guide on how to develop and nurture a gratitude mindset.

Daily Practices: Incorporate gratitude into your routine through simple, consistent habits.

a. **Gratitude Journaling**: Keeping a gratitude journal is a simple yet powerful practice that involves writing down things you're thankful for each day. This can be done in a physical notebook or a digital format.

Steps:

i) Set Aside Time: Dedicate a few minutes each day to reflect and write. This could be in the morning to start your day positively or at night to reflect on the day's highlights.

ii) Record Your Thoughts: Write down at least three things you're grateful for. These can range from significant events to small, everyday moments.

iii) Reflect: Take a moment to appreciate these aspects and how they positively impact your life.

Example: On a challenging day, you might write, "I'm grateful for the support of my family, the sunny weather, and the kindness of a stranger who held the door for me."

b. **Gratitude Rituals**: Incorporate gratitude into daily rituals or routines to make it a consistent practice.

Steps:

i) **Morning Affirmations**: Start your day with positive affirmations or a moment of reflection on what you're grateful for.

ii) **Gratitude at Meals**: Before meals, take a moment to express thanks for the food and the people who prepared it.

iii) **Evening Reflection**: End your day by listing things you're thankful for, either in a journal or through mental reflection.

Example: Before dinner, you might say, "I'm thankful for this meal, the effort of those who prepared it, and the company of my loved ones."

c. **Gratitude Reminders**: Use visual or auditory reminders to prompt moments of gratitude throughout the day.

Steps:

i) **Set Alarms**: Use phone alarms or reminders to prompt you to pause and reflect on something you're grateful for.

ii) **Visual Cues**: Place sticky notes or objects around your home or workspace that remind you to think about gratitude.

Example: Place a sticky note on your mirror that says, "Thank you for everything – for what I am grateful for today?" to prompt daily reflection.

Real life example of Gratitude:

Dr. Manjunath, our Mind Performance Coach, represents the practice of gratitude in every aspect of his life. He created a unique curriculum called the Gratitude Challenge, which has extremely changed the lives of his community members. This challenge has transformed their attitudes, teaching them to appreciate everything and everyone around them.

The simple act of saying, "Thank you for everything," has unlocked countless paths to joy and abundance, inner peace and happiness, growth and connection to the universe and whatnot. The power of gratitude is evident in Dr. Manjunath's life. Starting as a Software Engineer, he transformed into a Mind Performance Coach, guiding thousands of people across India. His secret lies in his unwavering attitude of gratitude.

In his daily life, Dr. Manjunath practices gratitude consistently. He expresses heartfelt thanks for every person and everything in his life, from a simple pin to the many blessings he has received. This practice is the foundation of his success, happiness, and inner peace.

A memorable moment occurred during the offline meet of Summit 2024. Dr. Manjunath, along with his community members, expressed gratitude to everyone who contributed to the summit's success. The atmosphere was filled with joy and thankfulness, leaving everyone inspired and united. This shared experience of gratitude brought a sense of harmony and positivity to all who attended.

From Dr. Manjunath's life example, we learn that an attitude of gratitude invites abundance into our lives without the need to pursue it. By embracing gratitude, things naturally fall into place, creating a life of positivity and peace. His ability to influence thousands of people through gratitude benefits not only individuals but also their families and the wider community.

Dr. Manjunath's journey shows us the power of gratitude to transform lives and build a positive society. By encouraging others to practice gratitude, he helps create a community based on appreciation and thankfulness, where everyone can thrive and grow together.

Practical Exercises for Cultivating Gratitude

Engaging in practical exercises helps reinforce the practice of gratitude, making it a more deep-rooted and natural part of daily life. Here are some detailed descriptions of exercises to nurture gratitude:

1. Gratitude Journaling

Purpose: Gratitude journaling is a powerful tool to shift your mindset towards positivity. By regularly acknowledging the things you're grateful for, you can foster a more appreciative and optimistic outlook on life.

Steps:

1. **Choose a Time**: Set aside a specific time each day for journaling, whether it's in the morning to start your day on a positive note, or in the evening to reflect on the day's blessings.
2. **Write Down Three Things**: Each day, write down at least three things you're grateful for. These can be big or small, from a supportive friend to the warmth of the sun. The key is to focus on the positive aspects of your life.
3. **Be Specific**: Instead of general statements, be specific about what you're grateful for. For example, instead of writing, "I'm grateful for my job," you might write, "I'm grateful for the encouraging feedback I received from my boss today."
4. **Reflect on Your Entries**: Occasionally, review your past entries. This can help you see patterns of positivity in your life and remind you of the good things, especially during challenging times.

Example: You might write, "Today, I'm grateful for the delicious cup of coffee I had this morning, the friendly chat with my neighbour, and the feeling of accomplishment after finishing a work project."

2. Gratitude Letters

Purpose: Writing gratitude letters allows you to express appreciation to those who have positively impacted your life. This practice not only strengthens relationships but also deepens your sense of gratitude.

Steps:

1. **Identify a Recipient**: Think of someone who has made a difference in your life, whether recently or in the past. This could be a friend, family member, mentor, or even a colleague.
2. **Write the Letter**: In your letter, express your gratitude by explaining how this person has positively impacted your life. Be specific about what they did and how it made you feel.
3. **Share or Keep**: You can choose to send the letter or keep it as a personal reflection. If you send it, the recipient will likely feel appreciated, which can strengthen your bond. If you keep it, the act of writing still helps reinforce your gratitude.

4. **Reflect**: After writing the letter, take a moment to reflect on the positive emotions that arise from expressing your gratitude. Notice how it shifts your mindset and deepens your appreciation.

Example: You might write a letter to an old teacher, expressing how their encouragement during a difficult time in school inspired you to pursue your dreams.

3. Mindful Appreciation

Purpose: Mindful appreciation is about being fully present in the moment and recognising the small joys in everyday life. This practice helps you cultivate an ongoing sense of gratitude by noticing the positive aspects of your environment and experiences.

Steps:

1. **Slow Down**: Throughout your day, take intentional pauses to notice the world around you. This could be during a walk, while eating, or simply sitting quietly.
2. **Focus on the Senses**: Engage your senses to enhance your awareness. For example, notice the vibrant colours of a sunset, the sound of birds chirping, or the taste of a delicious meal.
3. **Acknowledge the Moment**: Take a moment to mentally or verbally acknowledge what you appreciate about what you're experiencing. This

could be as simple as saying, "I'm grateful for this peaceful moment," or "I appreciate the warmth of the sun on my skin."

4. **Practice Regularly**: Incorporate mindful appreciation into your daily routine. The more you practice, the easier it becomes to find gratitude in the present moment.

Example: While drinking your morning coffee, take a moment to fully savour the aroma, the warmth of the mug in your hands, and the taste of the coffee. Acknowledge how these small moments contribute to your overall well-being.

By incorporating these practical exercises into your daily life, you can nurture a deeper sense of gratitude, leading to a more positive and fulfilling outlook.

By embracing gratitude, we open ourselves to greater joy, abundance, and inner peace, enriching our lives and those around us.

Points to remember

- **Gratitude Boosts Happiness**: Being thankful makes us happier and more content.
- **Gratitude Improves Health**: Practising gratitude can enhance both mental and physical well-being.
- **Gratitude Transforms Lives**: Small acts of gratitude lead to personal growth and success.
- **Gratitude Builds Strong Communities**: Sharing gratitude strengthens bonds and creates positive energy.
- **Gratitude Attracts Abundance**: A grateful mindset naturally brings more good into our lives.

Chapter 4

Love as Healing

"Love is the greatest healing power of all. It can mend the deepest wounds and bring light to the darkest places."

– Helen Keller

Love is a powerful force for healing and transformation. In this chapter, we explore how cultivating love for ourselves and others can bring about reflective change in our lives. The power of love resides within each of us every moment. This extraordinary energy is always available through our conscious recognition and choice to use it. When we decide to love one another, we rise above our limited perceptions and connect with a deeper truth, realising our unity, wholeness, and interconnectedness.

This kind of love is neither conditional nor something used to gain favours or seek validation. Instead, it is a universal and unconditional love that appreciates the beauty in life at every moment. It comes from a higher place within us, a natural expression that expects nothing in return and gives simply for the joy of giving. As we share and give love to others, we, in turn, receive the love we give. By expressing love to the world around us, the world mirrors back to us the true power of love.

Each of us wants to understand and experience this profound love. We search for it in our families, relationships, careers, passions, and in nature. All the while, the ability to experience and share this love lies within us, ready to be expressed and felt. Love is a powerful force, especially when it is shared.

1. Self-Love

Self-love is the foundation of a healthy and fulfilling life. It is about accepting yourself as you are, acknowledging your strengths and weaknesses, and treating yourself with kindness and respect. Self-love is not about being selfish or arrogant; it's about valuing yourself and your well-being.

Why is Self-Love Important?

Self-love plays a crucial role in leading a happy and balanced life. It's more than just a trend—it has a significant impact on our mental and physical well-being, as well as our relationships.

a. **Mental Health: Boosting Self-Esteem and Reducing Anxiety**

   Practising self-love helps improve self-esteem and confidence. When we accept ourselves, including our imperfections, we become more confident and content. Instead of being overly critical, we treat ourselves with compassion, which can reduce feelings of anxiety and depression. **For example**, when we love ourselves, we focus on our strengths and achievements rather than dwelling on our shortcomings. This positive mindset helps us feel less stressed and more capable of handling life's challenges.

b. **Physical Health: Caring for Our Bodies**

   Self-love encourages us to take better care of our bodies. When we truly value ourselves, we're more likely to make healthier choices, such as eating nutritious foods, exercising regularly, and getting enough sleep. Self-love involves listening to our bodies and taking steps to maintain our health. **For example**, someone who practices self-love might exercise because it makes them feel good, not just because they feel obligated. They might also choose to eat healthier foods because they want to nourish their body.

c. **Relationships: Establishing Healthy Boundaries and Attracting Respectful Connections**

   Self-love is vital for building healthy relationships. When we love ourselves, we set clear boundaries and expect others to treat us with respect. This helps us form relationships that are positive and supportive. Self-love also means we're less likely to tolerate negative behaviour from others. By practising self-love, we communicate our needs more effectively and build stronger, healthier relationships. We become more confident and secure, which helps us avoid unhealthy or toxic connections.

How to Cultivate Self-Love:

a) Practice Self-Care

Self-care involves engaging in activities that nourish your body and mind, helping you feel rejuvenated and balanced. Here are some ways you can incorporate self-care into your routine:

i. **Reading a Book:** Set aside 30 minutes each evening to read a book you enjoy. Create a cosy spot in your home with comfortable seating and good lighting to make this time enjoyable. For example, if you love mysteries, read a thrilling novel to unwind before bed.

ii. **Taking a Bath:** Dedicate one evening a week to a relaxing bath. Use soothing essential oils, bath salts, or bubbles to create a calming experience. Light a few candles and listen to soft music to enhance relaxation. For instance, if you're feeling stressed, a warm bath can be a perfect way to de-stress and recharge.

iii. **Going for a Walk:** Incorporate a daily walk into your routine, whether it's in a nearby park or around your neighbourhood. Aim for at least 20 minutes to enjoy the fresh air and clear your mind. If you're feeling overwhelmed at work, a short walk during lunch can provide a mental break and boost your mood.

b) Positive Affirmations

Positive affirmations help shift your mindset towards a more positive and supportive outlook. Here's how you can use them effectively:

i. **Morning Routine:** Start your day by repeating affirmations in front of the mirror. For example, say to yourself, "I am confident and capable" as you get ready for the day. This sets a positive tone for your day ahead.

ii. **Written Reminders:** Write down your favourite affirmations and place them in visible spots around your home, like on your bathroom mirror or your desk. For instance, write "I am deserving of happiness" on a sticky note and place it where you'll see it often.

iii. **Before Challenges:** Use affirmations before tackling challenging tasks or situations. If you're nervous about a presentation, remind yourself, "I am prepared and skilled" to boost your confidence and reduce anxiety.

c) Set Boundaries

Setting boundaries helps maintain your well-being and ensures that you're respecting your own limits. Here are some practical ways to set and maintain boundaries:

i. **At Work:** If you're frequently working overtime, set a clear end time for your workday. For example, decide that you will not check work emails after 6 PM. Communicate this boundary to your colleagues and stick to it to ensure you have time to relax and recharge.

ii. **With Friends and Family:** If you need time to yourself, let your loved ones know you need some personal space. For instance, if you're feeling overwhelmed, tell your family, "I need some quiet time to unwind. Let's catch up later."

iii. **In Social Settings:** If you're invited to events that you don't want to attend, it's okay to say no politely. For example, you can say, "I appreciate the invitation, but I have other plans that evening." This helps you avoid overcommitting and maintains your personal balance. By integrating these practices into your life, you create a healthier and more balanced routine, promoting self-love and overall well-being.

2. Unconditional Love

Once we cultivate self-love, we can more easily extend love and compassion to those around us. So turning the self-love into unconditional love is the everlasting deep connection with everyone.

Unconditional love is the purest form of love. It is a love that is given freely, without expectations or conditions. Unconditional love is accepting someone completely, flaws and all, and supporting them through their journey.

How to Cultivate Unconditional Love:

a. **Practice Empathy:** Empathy is the foundation of unconditional love, allowing you to connect deeply with others by understanding their thoughts, feelings, and experiences. When you practice empathy, you make an effort to see the world through someone else's eyes, which fosters deeper connections and strengthens relationships.

Family: In a family setting, empathy might mean understanding a sibling's struggles at school or work. Instead of criticising them for not meeting expectations, you listen and offer support, helping them navigate their challenges without judgement.

Friendship: If a friend is going through a tough time, like a breakup or job loss, practising empathy involves listening without interrupting or offering advice unless asked. You validate their feelings, showing them they're not alone in their experience.

Professional: In the workplace, empathy can be shown by recognising the stress a colleague is under during a tight deadline. Instead of pushing them harder, you offer to help or simply acknowledge their efforts, making them feel valued and supported.

b. **Let Go of Expectations:** Unconditional love means accepting people as they are, without trying to change them to fit your ideals or expectations. Letting go of expectations allows you to appreciate others for who they are, fostering a more genuine and loving relationship.

Family: Parents often have expectations for their children's future. Letting go of these expectations might mean accepting your child's decision to pursue a career that differs from what you envisioned and loving them for their unique path.

Friendship: In friendships, letting go of expectations might involve accepting that a friend doesn't always have time to meet up as frequently as you'd like. Instead of feeling hurt or disappointed, you value the time you do spend together and appreciate them for who they are.

Professional: In a professional context, letting go of expectations could mean accepting that a team member has a different working style than you. Instead of trying to change how they work, you focus on their strengths and support them in ways that align with their natural approach.

c. **Be Present:** Being present is about giving your full attention to the people you care about, showing them that they are important to you. This means actively listening, engaging in meaningful conversations, and being there for others in both good times and bad.

Family: In a family, being present could mean setting aside distractions like phones or work during family meals. You focus on enjoying each other's company and building a deeper connection through shared experiences.

Friendship: For friends, being present might involve checking in regularly, even when life gets busy. A simple message or call to see how they're doing shows that you care and are thinking of them, no matter how much time has passed.

Professional: At work, being present means truly listening to a colleague when they share their ideas or concerns during meetings. You give them your full attention, making them feel heard and respected, which strengthens your professional relationship.

By practising empathy, letting go of expectations, and being present, you cultivate unconditional love that enriches all areas of your life, from your family and friendships to your professional relationships.

The Interconnection between Self-Love and Unconditional Love

Self-love and unconditional love are deeply connected. When you love yourself, you are better equipped to love others unconditionally. Similarly, experiencing unconditional love from others can reinforce your self-love. Both forms of love contribute to a fulfilling and balanced life.

By embracing self-love and unconditional love, we can create a more compassionate and understanding world. Start by loving yourself, and you will naturally extend that love to others, fostering deeper connections and a more meaningful life.

Real life example:

Mohammad Rafiq, the founder of **Nasi Maa Foods** in Chennai, exemplifies how embracing self-love and practising unconditional love can transform an individual's life and positively impact the lives of those around him.

Discovering Purpose Through Self-Love

In his early years, Rafiq encountered numerous challenges, including low self-esteem and a lack of direction. Despite these obstacles, he remained determined to carve out his own path and achieve something significant. Rafiq realised that the first step towards success was to love and believe in himself.

Embarking on a journey of self-discovery, Rafiq learned to appreciate his own value and capabilities. He reflected on the struggle of finding quality home-cooked food during his bachelor years in Chennai and decided he wanted to support young people, the elderly, and anyone in need of nutritious meals. Rafiq spent time understanding his strengths and weaknesses, which helped him develop a sense of self-respect and confidence. This newfound self-love, combined with his desire to serve the community, inspired him to follow his passion for cooking and launch his own food business.

The Creation of Nasi Maa Foods

With a modest amount of savings, Rafiq established **Nasi Maa Foods**, a small eatery that offers home-style meals in Chennai. The name "Nasi Maa" was chosen to honour his mother, who instilled in him a love for cooking and served as his greatest inspiration. Rafiq's eating place quickly became popular due to its delicious food and welcoming atmosphere. He treated every customer as if they were part of his extended family, ensuring each meal was prepared with love and attention. Rafiq's dedication to his craft and the love he infused into his work resonated with the people of Chennai, turning **Nasi Maa Foods** into a beloved local favourite.

Extending Unconditional Love

Rafiq's journey wasn't just about establishing a successful business; it was also about making a positive difference in the community. He firmly believed that true success is measured by the impact one has on the lives of others. This belief led him to initiate various charitable activities through his business.

Every week, Rafiq organised free meal distributions for the underprivileged, making sure no one in his neighbourhood went hungry. He also created job opportunities for those in need, training them in culinary skills and helping them establish themselves in life.

Rafiq's kindness and generosity extended beyond his business endeavours. He actively participated in community events, supported local causes, and encouraged others to do the same. His steadfast commitment to helping others earned him immense love and respect within his community.

The Power of Love and Compassion

The success of **Nasi Maa Foods** and Rafiq's charitable efforts significantly impacted his life and the lives of those around him. His journey of self-love enabled him to find his true purpose and passion, while his unconditional love for others fostered a ripple effect of positivity and kindness within the community. Today, **Nasi Maa Foods** stands as more than just a popular eating place; it represents hope and compassion in Chennai. Mohammad Rafiq's story is a powerful testament to the transformative potential of self-love and unconditional love. His journey serves as a reminder that when we love ourselves and extend that love to others, we have the power to create a better world for everyone.

Practical exercises

a) Loving-Kindness Meditation

Loving-kindness meditation is a practice that involves focusing on sending love and positive wishes to yourself and others. This type of meditation helps cultivate compassion, empathy, and a sense of connection.

Steps:

i. **Find a Quiet Space:** Sit in a comfortable position in a quiet space where you won't be disturbed.

ii. **Close Your Eyes:** Gently close your eyes and take a few deep breaths to centre yourself.

iii. **Start with Yourself:** Begin by sending loving-kindness to yourself. Repeat silently or aloud: "May I be happy. May I be healthy. May I be safe. May I live with ease."

iv. **Expand to Others:** Gradually extend these wishes to others. Start with loved ones (family or friends), then move on to acquaintances, and finally, to people you find challenging. For each person, repeat: "May you be happy. May you be healthy. May you be safe. May you live with ease."

v. **Close the Meditation:** Conclude by bringing your focus back to yourself and wish yourself well once more. Take a few deep breaths and open your eyes by looking into your palm when you feel ready.

Example: You might visualise a close friend and say silently, "May you be surrounded by love and joy." This helps you foster a sense of warmth and goodwill towards others.

b) Daily Acts of Kindness

Daily acts of kindness involve doing small, thoughtful things for others. These acts can help reinforce feelings of love and compassion, benefiting both the giver and the receiver.

Steps:

i. **Identify Opportunities:** Look for simple ways to help others throughout your day. This could be as small as a smile, a compliment, or helping someone with a task.

ii. **Plan Your Acts:** Choose specific acts of kindness you can perform each day. For example, you might decide to compliment a coworker or offer to help a neighbour with groceries.

iii. **Perform the Acts:** Carry out your chosen acts with genuine intention. Smile at someone, hold the door open for a stranger, or send a kind message to a friend.

iv. **Reflect on the Impact:** After performing your acts of kindness, take a moment to reflect on how it felt. Notice any positive changes in your mood or interactions with others.

Example: You might bake cookies for a coworker who has been working hard or write a thank-you note to a friend who has been supportive.

c) Affirmations of Love.

Affirmations of love involve using positive statements to reinforce feelings of love and connection. These affirmations can help shift your mindset and deepen your sense of self-compassion and compassion for others.

Steps:

i. **Choose Affirmations:** Select affirmations that resonate with you and reflect the love and compassion you want to cultivate. Examples include, "I am worthy of love," or "I am connected with those around me."

ii. **Repeat Daily:** Incorporate these affirmations into your daily routine. You can say them aloud in front of a mirror, write them in a journal, or repeat them during meditation.

iii. **Visualise:** As you repeat your affirmations, visualise the positive feelings associated with them. Imagine yourself surrounded by love and extending that love to others.

iv. **Integrate into Life:** Use affirmations during moments of stress or self-doubt to reinforce your sense of love and connection. Remind yourself of these affirmations throughout the day as needed.

Example: If you're feeling disconnected from others, repeat, "I am loved and supported by those around me," while visualising positive interactions with people in your life.

Incorporating these exercises into your daily life can help you enhance your love and compassion, fostering a greater sense of connection and well-being.

Points to Remember:

- **Love Heals:** Love has the power to heal emotional wounds and bring positivity into our lives.
- **Unconditional Love:** True love doesn't expect anything in return; it simply supports and accepts others as they are.
- **Self-Love and Loving Others:** Loving yourself helps you love others better. When you care for yourself, you can genuinely care for others too.
- **Choosing Love:** Love is a choice you can make every day. By choosing love, you build deeper connections and a sense of togetherness.
- **Spreading Love:** When you show love, it inspires others to do the same, creating a kinder and more loving world.

Chapter 5

Applying Ho'oponopono in Daily Life

"In every moment, we have the power to choose love, forgiveness, and healing."

– Dr. Hew Len

Integrating Ho'oponopono into daily routines is a transformative practice that enhances mindfulness and fosters continuous healing. This ancient Hawaiian practice, rooted in forgiveness and reconciliation, offers profound benefits when applied to our everyday lives. By embracing Ho'oponopono principles, we can cultivate inner peace, address unresolved issues, and foster healthier relationships.

Ho'oponopono encourages us to take personal responsibility for our experiences and relationships, acknowledging that our thoughts, feelings, and actions play a role in shaping our reality. This practice invites us to engage in a cycle of cleansing and renewal, helping us to release negative patterns and embrace a more harmonious existence.

In this chapter, we will explore practical ways to unite Ho'oponopono into your daily life. We will cover actionable steps to incorporate its principles into your routines, relationships, and self-care practices. Whether you are new to Ho'oponopono or seeking to deepen your understanding, these practical applications will guide you in making this practice a natural and beneficial part of your life. By implementing these practices, you will enhance your awareness of the present moment, promote ongoing healing, and create a more balanced and fulfilling life. Embracing Ho'oponopono as a daily ritual not only supports personal growth but also nurtures a sense of connection and harmony with the world around you.

1. Mindful Living

Mindful living is about being present and intentional in every moment and applying Ho'oponopono. By integrating Ho'oponopono into your daily life, you align your actions with awareness and intentionality, fostering a more harmonious and fulfilling existence.

A. Cultivating Awareness through Ho'oponopono.

a) Daily Mindfulness Practice:

Begin with Presence: Start each day by grounding yourself in the present moment. Use deep breathing and mindful observation to centre your mind.

Apply Ho'oponopono Phrases: As you become aware of your thoughts and feelings, gently repeat the Ho'oponopono phrases: "I'm sorry. Please forgive me. Thank you. I love you." This practice helps you address and release any negative or unresolved emotions that arise throughout the day.

b) Mindful Observation:

Watch Your Thoughts: Observe your thoughts and reactions without judgement. When you notice negativity or distress, use the Ho'oponopono phrases to clear these feelings and return to a state of balance.

Acknowledge Triggers: Identify and acknowledge any situations or people that trigger negative emotions. Apply Ho'oponopono to these triggers to heal and transform your responses.

B. Intentional Living with Ho'oponopono

a) Setting Intentions:

Start with Purpose: Before beginning any task or interaction, set a clear and positive intention. For example, if you're starting a project, affirm: "I intend to approach this with clarity and positivity."

Incorporate Ho'oponopono: Infuse your intentions with the Ho'oponopono phrases to ensure they are aligned with forgiveness, love, and positivity. This helps in manifesting intentions that are pure and harmonious.

b) Mindful Actions:

Practice Presence: Focus fully on each activity you undertake. Whether you're working, interacting with others, or engaging in personal time, be fully present and mindful of your actions.

Respond with Love: Use Ho'oponopono to guide your responses. When faced with challenges or conflicts, approach them with a mindset of reconciliation and love, ensuring that your actions reflect your inner harmony.

C. Reflecting and Releasing

a) Daily Reflection:

End of Day Review: Before ending your day, take a few moments to reflect on your experiences. Consider how your intentions and actions aligned with your goals and values.

Ho'oponopono Reflection: Apply the Ho'oponopono phrases to any areas where you feel there may have been misalignment or where you seek healing. This practice helps in letting go of any lasting negativity and preparing for a new day with renewed clarity.

b) Continuous Improvement:

Seek Growth: Use your reflections to identify areas for personal growth and improvement. Set intentions for how you want to evolve and apply Ho'oponopono to support this growth.

Embrace Learning: Understand that mindful living is a continuous journey. Embrace each experience as an opportunity to learn and apply Ho'oponopono as a tool for ongoing self-awareness and intentional living.

D. Benefits of Applying Ho'oponopono in Mindful Living

a. **Enhanced Emotional Clarity:** Regular use of Ho'oponopono helps in clearing negative emotions, leading to a more balanced and centred emotional state.

b. **Improved Relationships:** By addressing and healing conflicts with Ho'oponopono, you foster healthier and more harmonious relationships.

c. **Greater Presence and Intentionality:** Integrating Ho'oponopono helps in aligning your actions with your intentions, leading to a more purposeful and mindful life.

d. **Ongoing Personal Growth:** The practice encourages continuous self-awareness and improvement, supporting a journey of personal development and fulfilment. Applying Ho'oponopono to mindful living involves integrating awareness and intentionality into your daily routine. By cultivating presence, setting clear intentions, and reflecting with the practice of forgiveness and love, you enhance your ability to live meaningfully and harmoniously. Embrace this approach to create a life that is both intentional and deeply connected to the values of forgiveness and unconditional love.

2. Building Habits

Create rituals and habits that reinforce the practice, making it a natural part of your daily routine.

A. Morning Rituals:

Start the day with reflection and setting intentions using the four key phrases.

a) Set Your Intention:

Begin your day by setting a positive intention. Reflect on what you wish to achieve or experience with a clear, positive mindset.

b) Grounding Exercise:

Take a few moments to ground yourself. Close your eyes, take deep breaths, and feel your connection to the earth. This helps in centring your mind and setting a calm tone for the day.

c) Ho'oponopono Affirmations:

Repeat the Ho'oponopono phrases: "I'm sorry. Please forgive me. Thank you. I love you." You can say these aloud or silently, focusing on each phrase's meaning. Visualise these words washing over any negative thoughts or emotions.

d) Visualise a Positive Day:

Picture yourself having a successful and harmonious day. Visualise you are handling challenges with ease and maintaining a positive attitude throughout.

e) Gratitude Practice:

Express gratitude for the new day and the opportunities it brings. Acknowledge specific things you are thankful for, whether they are related to your personal life, work, or general well-being.

B. Evening Rituals:

End the day by reviewing experiences and expressing gratitude.

a) Reflect on the Day:

Spend a few minutes reflecting on your day. Consider any events, interactions, or feelings that stood out. Acknowledge both positive experiences and any challenges you faced.

b) Ho'oponopono Healing:

Use the Ho'oponopono phrases again: "I'm sorry. Please forgive me. Thank you. I love you." Focus on any specific situations or people that caused you distress during the day. This practice helps in releasing any lingering negative emotions and healing relationships.

c) Self-Compassion:

Practice self-compassion by acknowledging your efforts and any growth you experienced. Recognise that it's okay to make mistakes and that you are deserving of love and forgiveness.

d) Affirmations of Peace:

Repeat affirmations that promote peace and relaxation. Phrases like "I am at peace" or "I let go of today's worries" can help you unwind and prepare for restful sleep.

e) Gratitude Review:

Reflect on the positive aspects of your day and express gratitude for them. Even if the day was challenging, finding moments of gratitude can shift your focus to a more positive perspective.

f) Prepare for Rest:

As you wind down, engage in calming activities such as reading, meditating, or listening to soothing music. Ensure your environment is conducive to a restful night's sleep.

3.Benefits of the Rituals

Morning Rituals:

- Start your day with clarity and intention.
- Promote a positive mindset and reduce stress.
- Enhance your ability to handle daily challenges.

Evening Rituals:

- Facilitate emotional healing and release negativity.
- Improve self-awareness and self-compassion.
- Promote relaxation and restful sleep.

By incorporating these morning and evening rituals into your daily routine, you can enhance your practice of Ho'oponopono, fostering a deeper sense of peace, clarity, and emotional well-being.

Practical Exercises:

Implement exercises to seamlessly integrate Ho'oponopono:

a. **Daily Mantras:** Use the Ho'oponopono phrases as mantras throughout the day to maintain focus and calm.

b. **Mindful Breathing:** Practice deep breathing while repeating the phrases to centre yourself during stressful moments.

c. **Gratitude Practice:** Incorporate moments of gratitude into everyday activities, such as clothes, shelter, meals, or walks.

Points to Remember:

- **Stay Mindful**: Use Ho'oponopono throughout the day to stay present and release negative emotions.
- **Start with Positive Intentions**: Begin each day by setting positive goals, guided by love and forgiveness.
- **Reflect Daily**: End your day by reflecting and letting go of any negativity using Ho'oponopono.
- **Build Healing Habits**: Create simple morning and evening routines that include Ho'oponopono phrases and gratitude.
- **Use Practical Tools**: Incorporate Ho'oponopono into your day with easy practices like repeating the phrases, deep breathing, and expressing gratitude.

Chapter 6

Transforming Relationships

"The quality of your life is determined by the quality of your relationships."

– Tony Robbins

Ho'oponopono provides a deep framework for healing and strengthening our connections with others, offering tools to promote deeper, more meaningful relationships. At its core, Ho'oponopono is a practice of reconciliation and forgiveness, guiding us to take responsibility for our role in relationships and encouraging us to address conflicts and misunderstandings with a compassionate heart.

In this chapter, we explore how Ho'oponopono can be applied to transform relationships, whether they are with family, friends, colleagues, or even ourselves. By embracing the principles of Ho'oponopono—such as personal responsibility, forgiveness, and letting go of judgement—we can address underlying issues, heal emotional wounds, and build stronger, more authentic connections.

We will explore practical strategies for applying Ho'oponopono in various relational contexts, from resolving conflicts and enhancing communication to nurturing trust and empathy. Through this exploration, you'll learn how to use Ho'oponopono to create a more harmonious and supportive network of relationships.

By integrating these principles into your interactions, you will not only improve your relationships but also enrich your life with deeper bonds and mutual understanding. Embracing Ho'oponopono as a tool for transformation will help you cultivate relationships that are grounded in love, respect, and genuine connection.

1. Healing Dynamics

Understanding and addressing the underlying issues in relationships is essential for genuine healing and transformation. This process involves several key practices:

A. Open Communication:

Encouraging honest and empathetic dialogue is crucial for resolving conflicts and rebuilding connections. Open communication involves:

Expressing Needs and Feelings: Share your thoughts and emotions openly and honestly, without fear of judgement or retaliation.

Seeking Common Ground: Focus on finding mutual understanding and solutions rather than placing blame.

Creating Safe Spaces: Foster an environment where all parties feel comfortable expressing themselves without fear of criticism.

B. Active Listening:

Active listening helps in truly hearing and validating others' perspectives, which is vital for building trust and fostering deeper connections. Key aspects include:

Full Attention: Give your complete focus to the speaker, avoiding interruptions and distractions.

Empathetic Responses: Acknowledge and validate the speaker's feelings and viewpoints, showing understanding and empathy.

Clarification: Ask questions of what has been said to ensure accurate understanding and avoid misunderstandings.

By integrating these practices into your relationships, you can address and resolve underlying issues, promote healing, and create more meaningful and harmonious connections.

2. Creating Connections

Applying the principles of Ho'oponopono to foster meaningful and lasting connections involves cultivating empathy, mutual respect, and a deep understanding of others. This approach not only enriches relationships but also builds a foundation for harmonious interactions.

Empathy and Understanding

Cultivate Empathy: Empathy involves deeply connecting with others by understanding their feelings, experiences, and perspectives. The practice of Ho'oponopono—focusing on forgiveness, love, and gratitude—can significantly enhance our ability to empathise, bridging gaps between individuals and fostering genuine relationships. Here's how to cultivate empathy in family, friendships, and professional settings:

a) Put Yourself in Others' Shoes

Putting yourself in others' shoes is a fundamental aspect of cultivating empathy. This principle involves stepping outside of your own experiences and perspectives to truly understand and appreciate the feelings and thoughts of those around you. By viewing situations from another person's vantage point, you gain insights into their emotions, challenges, and motivations, leading to more compassionate and meaningful interactions.

In the context of Ho'oponopono, this practice aligns with the philosophy of taking responsibility not only for your own actions but also for how you perceive and respond to others. It encourages a deep connection with those around you, fostering a sense of unity and shared experience.

Putting yourself in others' shoes allows you to respond to situations with a more open heart, reducing conflict and fostering deeper connections. It helps you to move beyond judgement and assumptions, creating space for healing, understanding, and the strengthening of relationships.

The examples below will help you understand and apply through your own personal journey:

Family Relationships: If your teenage son has been spending a lot of time in his room and seems distant, instead of assuming he is being rebellious or uninterested in family activities, try to understand his perspective. Consider that he might be dealing with stress from school, peer pressure, or personal insecurities. Reflect on the Ho'oponopono phrases to approach the situation with empathy: "I'm sorry. Please forgive me. Thank you. I love you."

Illustration: "When your son spends most of his time alone in his room, it's easy to think he's avoiding the family. But by putting yourself in his shoes, you might see that he's struggling with school stress or social anxiety. Understanding this can help you support him better."

Friendship: Imagine you have a friend who has been unusually quiet and withdrawn lately. Instead of thinking they are being distant or uninterested in your friendship, consider their perspective. They might be dealing with personal issues or going through a challenging time. Using the Ho'oponopono approach, silently repeat the phrases, "I'm sorry. Please forgive me. Thank you. I love you," to help you approach your friend with empathy and compassion.

Illustration: "When your friend starts pulling away, it's natural to feel hurt or confused. But by stepping into their shoes, you may discover they're facing personal challenges that are hard to talk about. Understanding their situation can help you be a better friend and offer the support they need."

Professional Environment: As a manager, if one of your team members is frequently late to meetings, rather than assuming they are irresponsible, try to understand their perspective. They might have personal challenges, such as a difficult family situation or unreliable transportation, impacting their punctuality. Reflect on the Ho'oponopono phrases, "I'm sorry. Please forgive me. Thank you. I love you," to approach the situation with empathy and understanding.

Illustration: "Understanding why a colleague is consistently late to meetings—rather than labelling them as unprofessional—can reveal underlying issues. If you see things from their perspective, you might find that their slowness is due to personal challenges they are facing, not a lack of respect for your time."

b) Acknowledge Different Experiences

Acknowledging different experiences is a key component of empathy and understanding in the Ho'oponopono practice. This principle involves recognising that each person's behaviour, beliefs, and reactions are shaped by their unique life experiences. By honouring these differences, you create a foundation for deeper connections and mutual respect.

In the Ho'oponopono tradition, acknowledging different experiences means accepting that everyone's journey is distinct. Just as you have faced challenges, learned lessons, and developed your worldview, so have others. This awareness helps you to approach interactions with an open mind and heart, reducing the likelihood of misunderstandings and judgements.

Acknowledging different experiences is about seeing the value in diversity and using that understanding to build more harmonious and supportive relationships. It allows you to move beyond surface-level interactions and connect with others on a deeper, more meaningful level, promoting healing and growth for everyone involved.

c) Respond with Compassion

Responding with compassion is an essential aspect of transforming relationships through the principles of Ho'oponopono. Compassion involves approaching every interaction with kindness, understanding, and a genuine desire to support and uplift others. It's about being present in the moment, recognising the emotions of those around you, and responding in a way that nurtures healing and connection.

In Ho'oponopono, responding with compassion means that you not only acknowledge the experiences and feelings of others but also actively choose to interact in a way that brings comfort and resolution. This practice helps to dissolve negativity, ease tensions, and foster a supportive environment where relationships can thrive.

Responding with compassion, guided by the Ho'oponopono principles, allows you to interact with others in a way that promotes healing, understanding, and growth. It creates a ripple effect of kindness, transforming not just your relationships but also the environments in which you live and work.

Below are examples where you will be able to manage similar situations in your life:

Family Relationships: During a heated argument with a family member about a misunderstanding, instead of reacting defensively, take a moment to express empathy. You might say, "I understand that this situation has upset you, and I'm truly sorry for my part in it. Let's talk about how we can resolve this together." Using the Ho'oponopono phrases, "I'm sorry. Please forgive me. Thank you. I love you," helps to heal and strengthen the relationship.

Illustration: "Responding to a family member's distress with compassion—by acknowledging their feelings and offering a sincere apology—demonstrates that you value their emotions and are committed to resolving the conflict with kindness. This approach fosters a supportive and understanding family environment."

Friendship: If a friend is upset about something you said or did, instead of becoming defensive or dismissive, respond with compassion. Apologise sincerely and offer to listen to their concerns. For example, you might say, "I'm sorry for what happened. I didn't mean to hurt you. Let's talk about it." The Ho'oponopono phrases, "I'm sorry. Please forgive me. Thank you. I love you," guide you to respond with empathy and understanding.

Illustration: "When a friend expresses hurt or frustration, responding with compassion—by acknowledging their feelings and offering a heartfelt apology—shows that you value their emotions and are committed to repairing the relationship. This act of empathy strengthens the bond of friendship."

Professional Environment: When a colleague comes to you with a concern or complaint, instead of dismissing their feelings or concerns, show compassion by listening attentively and acknowledging their perspective. Offer your support and understanding to help address the issue. Reflect on the Ho'oponopono phrases, "I'm sorry. Please forgive me. Thank you. I love you," to approach the situation with kindness and empathy.

Illustration: "When a colleague shares a concern or complaint, responding with compassion—by listening to their perspective and offering support—demonstrates that you value their input and are committed to finding a resolution together. This approach fosters a respectful and collaborative work environment."

By integrating these principles, you can build meaningful and enduring connections, creating a supportive and harmonious environment in both personal and professional relationships.

3. Benefits of Transforming Relationships with Ho'oponopono

a. **Enhanced Communication:** Applying Ho'oponopono principles, such as empathy and active listening, leads to more effective and meaningful conversations. When you encourage open communication, express your needs and feelings without fear of judgement, and seek common ground, you create an environment where all parties feel heard and understood. This fosters a deeper connection and allows for the resolution of conflicts in a way that strengthens relationships.

b. **Deeper Understanding:** By putting yourself in others' shoes and acknowledging different experiences, you develop a profound understanding of one another's needs and concerns. Ho'oponopono encourages you to move beyond your own perspective and consider the emotions, challenges, and motivations of others. This deepened understanding builds trust and helps to bridge gaps in relationships, making it easier to navigate difficult conversations and situations.

c. **Stronger Bonds:** Responding with compassion and practising mutual respect creates a sense of closeness and trust that strengthens relationships. When you consistently approach interactions with kindness, validate others' feelings, and honour personal boundaries, you build a foundation of respect and love. These practices, rooted in Ho'oponopono, not only heal existing wounds but also prevent future conflicts, resulting in more meaningful and enduring connections in both personal and professional settings.

These benefits highlight the transformative power of Ho'oponopono in relationships. By fostering open communication, deepening understanding, and strengthening bonds, you create a supportive and harmonious environment where all relationships can thrive.

Practical Exercises

Engage in exercises to enhance relationship dynamics:

a. **Family Dialogues:** Initiate structured conversations with family members using Ho'oponopono principles to address and heal conflicts. Focus on open communication, empathy, and mutual respect to resolve issues and strengthen bonds.

b. **Conflict Resolution Role-Playing:** Practice resolving disputes constructively through role-playing scenarios. This exercise helps you develop the skills needed to handle real-life conflicts with empathy and understanding.

c. **Shared Gratitude Practices:** Encourage family or group gratitude sessions to strengthen relationships. Expressing gratitude together fosters a sense of unity and appreciation, enhancing the overall harmony within the group.

Points to Remember

- **Heal Relationships**: Use Ho'oponopono to openly communicate and listen, helping to resolve conflicts and heal emotional wounds.
- **Practice Empathy**: Understand others by putting yourself in their shoes, recognising their experiences, and responding with kindness.
- **Show Respect**: Build strong relationships by respecting others' feelings and ensuring everyone feels valued and heard.
- **Improve Communication**: Apply Ho'oponopono to communicate better, listen actively, and find common ground to strengthen connections.
- **Practical Exercises**: Try family talks, role-playing conflicts, and sharing gratitude to improve and strengthen relationships.

Chapter 7

Inner Peace and Personal Growth

"Peace comes from within. Do not seek it without."

– Buddha

"Personal growth is not a matter of changing who you are, but of becoming who you truly are."

– Marianne Williamson

Achieving inner peace is an ongoing journey, one that requires consistent self-reflection, managing emotions, and connecting the mind and body. In a world full of constant change and pressures, finding this inner calm can be challenging. However, Ho'oponopono offers a valuable path to help you achieve balance. Rooted in the principles of forgiveness, responsibility, and love, this practice provides practical tools to help you handle life's challenges with clarity and peace.

Ho'oponopono goes beyond just resolving conflicts or healing relationships; it's a deep spiritual practice that encourages personal growth and self-discovery. By engaging in this practice, you begin to remove the negative emotions, limiting beliefs, and habitual behaviours that block your path to true inner peace. You learn to take responsibility for your thoughts and actions, empowering yourself to create a life of harmony and balance.

This chapter explores how Ho'oponopono can transform your journey towards inner peace and support your personal growth. It looks at key areas like emotional regulation, the mind-body connection, and the process of self-discovery. Through these insights, you'll learn how to cultivate a sense of inner silence that not only improves your well-being but also positively impacts your relationships with others and the world around you.

The journey to inner peace isn't a final destination but an ongoing process of growth and learning. As you embrace the principles of Ho'oponopono, you'll find that inner peace becomes more attainable, even in the face of life's challenges. This chapter serves as a guide to help you integrate these practices into your daily life, leading to a more centred, balanced, and fulfilling existence.

1. Peacefulness and Harmony.

Cultivating inner peace involves finding harmony within ourselves and our surroundings.

a) Emotional Regulation:

Emotional regulation is the ability to manage and respond to emotional experiences in a balanced and constructive way. Ho'oponopono emphasises taking responsibility for your emotions and using forgiveness, love, and gratitude to navigate through challenging feelings. This practice helps you gain control over your emotional responses, reducing stress and promoting inner peace.

Family: Imagine a situation where a family member's comment triggers feelings of anger or hurt. Instead of reacting impulsively, take a moment to breathe and mentally repeat the Ho'oponopono phrases: "I'm sorry. Please forgive me. Thank you. I love you." This process allows you to calm down and approach the situation with a clearer mind, leading to a more constructive and peaceful conversation.

Professional Setting: In a high-pressure work environment, it's easy to become overwhelmed by stress and frustration. When you feel these emotions rising, pause and apply the Ho'oponopono practice. Acknowledge the emotions without judgement and silently recite the phrases to help centre yourself. This technique not only aids in managing stress but also helps you maintain professionalism and clarity in your interactions.

b) Mind-Body Connection.

The mind-body connection is the understanding that physical well-being directly impacts mental and emotional health. Ho'oponopono encourages practices that nurture both the body and mind, recognising that a healthy body supports a peaceful mind. By aligning your physical habits with your mental and emotional needs, you create a holistic approach to well-being.

Family: Consider incorporating daily physical activities, like a family walk or yoga session, as part of your routine. These activities not only promote physical health but also serve as a bonding experience that enhances emotional connection. During these activities, practice mindfulness and describe Ho'oponopono phrases, reinforcing the mind-body connection and fostering a sense of peace and unity within the family.

2. Personal Growth

Consider how you handle stress. You might notice a pattern of procrastination or self-criticism when faced with challenges. Recognising this, you can use Ho'oponopono to address the underlying fears or insecurities driving this behaviour. By acknowledging these patterns, you create space for new, healthier habits to form, such as proactive planning or positive self-talk. These practices of emotional regulation and nurturing the mind-body connection help create a foundation for inner peace and personal growth, aligning with the holistic principles of Ho'oponopono.

a) Self-Discovery

Self-discovery is the process of exploring and understanding your true self—your thoughts, feelings, desires, and motivations. Ho'oponopono, with its focus on forgiveness, responsibility, and love, provides a framework for deep self-reflection. This practice encourages you to look within, recognise patterns that no longer serve you, and embrace the changes necessary for personal growth. Through this journey, you uncover your authentic self, leading to greater self-awareness and fulfilment.

b) Identifying Patterns

Identifying patterns involves recognising recurring thoughts, emotions, and behaviours that may be limiting your potential or hindering personal growth. These patterns can be deeply ingrained, often formed by past experiences, beliefs, or societal expectations.

Ho'oponopono helps in bringing these patterns to light, allowing you to consciously choose to change them.

Family: In family interactions, you may notice that you often react with frustration when a particular topic is brought up. By practising Ho'oponopono, you can begin to identify the underlying cause of this reaction. Perhaps it's rooted in a past conflict or unresolved emotions. Through self-reflection and the use of the Ho'oponopono phrases—"I'm sorry. Please forgive me. Thank you. I love you."—you can start to release these old patterns and respond in a more loving and constructive way.

Consider how you handle stress. You might notice a pattern of procrastination or self-criticism when faced with challenges. Recognising this, you can use Ho'oponopono to address the underlying fears or insecurities driving this behaviour. By acknowledging these patterns, you create space for new, healthier habits to form, such as proactive planning or positive self-talk.

c) Embracing Change

Embracing change is about fostering a mindset that is open to transformation, new experiences, and growth. Change can be challenging, often met with resistance or fear, but it is also essential for personal development. Ho'oponopono encourages you to accept change as a natural and beneficial part of life, helping you move forward with confidence and grace.

Family: Imagine an important change in your family, such as a child leaving home for college, a daughter leaving home after getting married, or a spouse retiring. These transitions can be emotionally charged and unsettling. Through Ho'oponopono, you can embrace these changes by focusing on gratitude for the experiences shared and the new opportunities that lie ahead. The phrases, "I'm sorry. Please forgive me. Thank you. I love you," can be used to process emotions and accept the new phase of life with an open heart.

Professional Setting: In your career, embracing change might involve taking on a new role or adapting to a shift in company culture. Initially, this change might bring discomfort or doubt. However, by applying Ho'oponopono, you can approach the situation with a mindset of growth and learning. Use the practice to release fears and trust in your ability to adapt, recognising that change often brings new opportunities for success and fulfilment.

Thus, incorporating Ho'oponopono into the journey of self-discovery allows you to recognise and transform limiting patterns while embracing the changes that lead to personal growth. By exploring your inner world with compassion and openness, you uncover your true self and create a life that reflects your authentic values and desires.

Practical Exercises

Engaging in practical exercises can significantly enhance your journey towards inner peace and personal growth. These activities are designed to help you apply the principles of Ho'oponopono and develop a deeper sense of silence and self-discovery.

a) Visualisation Techniques

Visualisation involves using guided imagery to create a mental picture of a desired outcome or state of being. This technique can help you relax and focus on personal goals by vividly imagining them as if they are already achieved.

How to Practice:

i. **Find a Quiet Space:** Sit or lie down in a comfortable position in a quiet space where you won't be disturbed.

ii. **Close Your Eyes:** Take a few deep breaths to centre yourself and relax.

iii. **Create Your Vision:** Picture a calm place or a situation where you feel completely at peace and fulfilled. Imagine every detail—what you see, hear, and feel in that space.

iv. **Focus on Your Goals:** Visualise yourself achieving your personal goals. Picture the steps you need to take, the feelings of accomplishment, and the positive impact on your life.

v. **Repeat Regularly:** Practice this exercise daily or as needed to reinforce your goals and maintain a sense of calm and focus.

Example: If you're feeling stressed about a career change, visualise yourself confidently navigating the transition. Imagine the new opportunities, the positive interactions with colleagues, and the satisfaction of achieving your professional goals.

b) Meditative Practices

Meditation involves focusing your mind and calming your thoughts through various techniques. Daily meditation can help you centre your thoughts, reduce stress, and cultivate a sense of inner peace.

How to Practice:

i. **Choose a Meditation Style:** Select a meditation technique that resonates with you, such as mindfulness, forgiveness meditation, or loving-kindness meditation.

ii. **Set a Time:** Dedicate a specific time each day for meditation, even if it's just 5-10 minutes.

iii. **Find a Comfortable Position:** Sit comfortably with your back straight. You can sit on a chair, cushion, or floor.

iv. **Focus Your Attention:** Concentrate on your breath, a mantra, or a guided meditation. Gently bring your attention back whenever your mind wanders.

v. **Reflect on Your Practice:** After meditation, take a moment to reflect on how you feel and any insights gained.

Example: Begin each day with a 10-minute mindfulness meditation. Focus on your breath and observe your thoughts without judgement. This practice can help you start the day with a clear mind and a sense of calm.

c) Goal-Setting Workshops

Goal-setting workshops involve setting clear intentions and creating actionable plans for personal development. These workshops help you identify your goals, break them down into manageable steps, and track your progress.

How to Practice:

i. **Define Your Goals:** Identify specific, measurable, attainable, relevant, and time-bound (SMART) goals you want to achieve.

ii. **Create an Action Plan:** Break down each goal into smaller, actionable steps. Outline the tasks needed to achieve each step and set deadlines.

iii. **Review and Adjust:** Regularly review your progress and adjust your plans as needed. Celebrate milestones and reassess your goals to ensure they align with your evolving needs.

iv. **Accountability Partner:** Consider working with a coach or accountability partner to stay motivated and on track.

Example: If your goal is to improve your physical fitness, set specific targets like attending a fitness class three times a week. Create a plan with steps such as scheduling workouts, tracking your progress, and adjusting your routine based on your performance.

Points to Remember:

- **Emotional Balance**: Ho'oponopono helps you manage emotions like stress and anger, leading to a calmer and more peaceful mind.
- **Mind-Body Harmony**: Recognise that a healthy body supports a peaceful mind. Daily activities like walking or meditation can enhance both physical and mental well-being.
- **Self-Discovery**: Use Ho'oponopono to explore and understand your true self, identifying and changing old patterns that hold you back.
- **Embrace Change**: Approach life changes with an open heart, using Ho'oponopono to release fears and grow from new experiences.
- **Practical Techniques**: Apply daily practices like visualisation and meditation to reinforce your journey toward inner peace and personal growth.

Chapter 8

Your Practice Guide

"Small daily improvements over time lead to stunning results."

– Robin Sharma

The chapter is dedicated to providing a clear and actionable roadmap for integrating Ho'oponopono into your daily life. This chapter serves as a practical guide, outlining the essential steps to begin or deepen your practice of this transformative Hawaiian tradition. Whether you are a beginner or an experienced practitioner, the aim is to offer structured guidance that can help you effectively apply Ho'oponopono principles to foster healing, enhance relationships, and cultivate inner peace.

This chapter is divided into three parts: one for the beginners, another for the advanced practitioners, and practical exercises for your ready reference.

1. Beginner Techniques

Embarking on your Ho'oponopono journey can be both exciting and transformative. For those new to the practice, starting with foundational exercises can help ease into the process and build a strong base. This section provides detailed descriptions and steps for two fundamental techniques:

A. Creating a Practice Space

A dedicated practice space provides a calm environment that supports reflection, meditation, and the overall Ho'oponopono experience. This space is crucial for cultivating a sense of peace and commitment to your practice.

Steps:

a) Choose a Quiet Location:

Find a space in your home where you can be undisturbed. It should be quiet, comfortable, and free from distractions. This could be a corner of a room, a spare room, or even a section of your living area.

b) Set Up the Space:

Comfort: Ensure the space has comfortable seating, such as a cushion, chair, or mat. The seating should support relaxation and proper posture.

Ambiance: Create a calm atmosphere using soft lighting, soothing colours, and calming decorations. Consider adding elements like candles, plants, or crystals to enhance the environment.

Personal Touches: Include items that inspire you or that you associate with peace and reflection, such as inspirational quotes or artwork.

c) Maintain Cleanliness and Order:

Keep the space tidy and organised. A clean environment helps maintain focus and clarity during your practice.

d) Incorporate Tools:

Have any tools or materials you might need, such as a journal, meditation cushion, or essential oils, readily available in this space.

e) Set a Routine:

Dedicate specific times each day to use this space for your Ho'oponopono practice. Consistency helps reinforce the habit and deepens the practice.

Example: Imagine creating a small corner of your living room with a comfortable chair, soft lighting, and a few inspirational items. Each morning, you sit in this space, take a few deep breaths, and begin your Ho'oponopono practice, gradually building a daily routine that feels natural and inviting.

B. Daily Rituals

Daily rituals help integrate Ho'oponopono into your everyday life, making it a consistent and meaningful part of your routine. Starting with simple practices can build familiarity and reinforce the principles of Ho'oponopono.

Steps:

a) Start with Key Phrases:

The core of Ho'oponopono involves four key phrases: "I'm sorry," "Please forgive me," "Thank you," and "I love you." Begin by incorporating these phrases into your daily routine.

b) Set a Specific Time:

Choose a specific time each day for your Ho'oponopono practice. This could be in the morning, during a break, or before bed. Consistency is key to forming a lasting habit.

c) Begin with Short Sessions:

Start with short practice sessions, such as 5-10 minutes. Focus on repeating the phrases silently or aloud and reflect on their meaning and significance.

d) Incorporate Reflection:

Use your practice time to reflect on specific situations, emotions, or relationships where you seek healing or resolution. Direct the phrases toward these areas to facilitate personal growth.

e) Use a Journal:

Keep a journal to record your thoughts, feelings, and insights during your practice. Writing down your experiences can enhance self-awareness and track your progress.

f) Gradually Expand:

As you become more comfortable with the practice, consider extending your sessions or incorporating additional elements such as meditation or visualisation into your routine.

Example: Begin each day by sitting in your designated practice space. Spend a few minutes repeating the phrases "I'm sorry,", "Please forgive me,", "Thank you,", and "I love you." Reflect on any areas of your life where you seek improvement or healing, and jot down your reflections in your journal.

By starting with these foundational techniques, you create a solid framework for your Ho'oponopono practice. These beginner steps will help you ease into the practice, build consistency, and gradually deepen your experience, paving the way for more advanced techniques and a richer understanding of Ho'oponopono.

2. Advanced Practices

For those who have established a foundational Ho'oponopono practice and wish to deepen their experience, advanced techniques offer opportunities for further growth and exploration. These practices build upon the basics and introduce more complex methods to enhance the depth and effectiveness of your Ho'oponopono journey.

A. In-Depth Meditations

In-depth meditations involve extended sessions that delve deeply into specific aspects of Ho'oponopono, such as forgiveness, gratitude, and personal healing. These meditations allow you to explore and integrate the principles of Ho'oponopono on a deeper level.

Steps:

a) Prepare Your Space:

Ensure that your practice space is favourable to extended meditation. It should be comfortable, quiet, and free from interruptions.

b) Set an Intention:

Before starting, set a clear intention for your meditation. Decide which aspect of Ho'oponopono you wish to focus on, such as forgiveness of yourself or others, or cultivating gratitude.

c) Begin with Relaxation:

Start by taking several deep breaths to relax your body and mind. Focus on calming any tension and clearing your mind of distractions.

d) Guided Imagery:

Use guided imagery to visualise specific scenarios related to your intention. For example, if focusing on forgiveness, imagine yourself and the person you wish to forgive in a peaceful setting. Visualise the healing process as you repeat the Ho'oponopono phrases.

e) Extended Reflection:

Spend a longer period (15-30 minutes) reflecting deeply on the chosen aspect. Allow thoughts and emotions to surface without judgement. Use the Ho'oponopono phrases as a tool to process and release these feelings.

f) Integration:

Conclude the meditation by integrating the experience. Take a moment to reflect on any insights gained and how they can be applied to your daily life.

Example: If you are working on self-forgiveness, you might spend 20 minutes visualising yourself in a supportive and loving environment, facing past mistakes with compassion. Repeat the phrases "I'm sorry," "Please forgive me," "Thank you," and "I love you," as you mentally work through these emotions and visualise healing.

B. Integrative Exercises

Integrative exercises combine Ho'oponopono with other mindfulness or spiritual practices to create a more comprehensive approach to personal growth and healing. This fusion enhances the overall effects of the practices and supports a more holistic experience.

Steps:

a) Select Complementary Practices:

Choose mindfulness or spiritual practices that resonate with you, such as yoga, journaling, or breathwork. Ensure that these practices align with the principles of Ho'oponopono and support your goals.

b) Combine Practices:

Integrate Ho'oponopono phrases into your chosen practice. For example, if practising yoga, repeat the Ho'oponopono phrases during specific poses or sequences. In journaling, use the phrases as prompts to explore your thoughts and feelings.

c) Create a Routine:

Develop a routine that incorporates both Ho'oponopono and the complementary practices. For instance, you might start your day with a brief Ho'oponopono meditation, followed by a yoga session that incorporates affirmations related to your intentions.

d) Monitor Your Experience:

Pay attention to how combining practices affect your overall well-being. Notice any changes in your emotional state, mental clarity, or physical health. Adjust your routine as needed to optimise the benefits.

e) Reflect and Adapt:

Regularly reflect on the effectiveness of the integrated practices. Adapt and refine your approach based on your experiences and insights.

Example: Combine Ho'oponopono with breathwork by performing a series of deep breathing exercises while silently repeating the phrases. This combination can enhance relaxation and emotional release. Alternatively, integrate Ho'oponopono into a journaling practice by writing about specific situations and using the phrases to guide your reflections and healing process.

These advanced practices allow you to deepen your Ho'oponopono journey by exploring more complex techniques and combining them with other mindfulness practices. By engaging in in-depth meditations and integrative exercises, you enhance your ability to achieve inner peace, foster personal growth, and experience the transformative power of Ho'oponopono in a more profound way.

Practical Exercises

To make the most out of Ho'oponopono, it's important to tailor practices to your individual needs and circumstances. Incorporating personalised routines and adapting techniques can ensure that Ho'oponopono becomes a natural and effective part of your daily life.

a) Personalised Routine

Creating a personalised routine involves integrating Ho'oponopono practices into your daily life in a way that suits your specific schedule, preferences, and goals. This routine helps establish consistency and ensures that Ho'oponopono becomes a meaningful and sustainable part of your life.

Steps:

i) Assess Your Schedule:

Begin by evaluating your daily routine and identifying available time slots for Ho'oponopono practices. Consider your work hours, family commitments, and personal time.

ii) Set Clear Goals:

Define what you want to achieve with your Ho'oponopono practice. Goals might include reducing stress, improving relationships, or fostering personal growth.

iii) Choose Practices:

Select specific Ho'oponopono practices that align with your goals. This might include meditation, affirmations, or visualisation exercises. Choose practices that resonate with you and fit well into your schedule.

iv) Create a Schedule:

Develop a daily or weekly schedule that includes time for your chosen Ho'oponopono practices. For example, you might allocate 10 minutes each morning for meditation and 5 minutes before bed for affirmations.

v) Incorporate Flexibility:

Allow for flexibility in your routine to accommodate changes in your life. If you miss a session, simply adjust your schedule rather than feeling discouraged.

vi) Track Your Progress:

Keep a journal to track your practice and reflect on any changes or benefits you experience. This helps maintain motivation and provides insights into what works best for you.

Example: If you work long hours and have a busy family life, you might schedule a 5-minute Ho'oponopono meditation in the morning before starting your day, and a brief reflection session in the evening before bed. Adjust these times as needed based on your daily demands and commitments.

b) Adapting Techniques

Adapting techniques involves modifying Ho'oponopono exercises to fit your evolving needs and circumstances. This flexibility ensures that the practices remain relevant and effective as your life changes.

Steps:

i) Identify Changing Needs:

Regularly assess your current life situation and emotional needs. Identify any new challenges or goals that may require adjustments to your Ho'oponopono practice.

ii) Modify Practices:

Based on your assessment, modify the techniques you use. For example, if you're facing a new personal challenge, you might focus more on forgiveness practices or increase the frequency of meditation sessions.

iii) Experiment with Variations:

Try different variations of Ho'oponopono practices to see what works best for your current situation. This might include changing the format of your affirmations, exploring new meditation styles, or integrating Ho'oponopono with other wellness practices.

iv) Seek Feedback:

Reflect on how the changes affect your well-being. Seek feedback from yourself and, if appropriate, from others who support your practice. Use this feedback to make further adjustments.

v) Stay Open to Change:

Embrace the idea that your practice may need to evolve over time. Be open to experimenting with new techniques or adjusting existing ones to better meet your needs.

vi) Incorporate New Insights:

As you adapt your practices, incorporate any new insights or techniques you find helpful. Continuously refine your approach to keep it aligned with your personal growth and changing circumstances.

Example: If you find that your initial meditation practice no longer feels as effective due to increased stress at work, you might adapt by extending the meditation sessions or incorporating guided imagery to address specific stressors. Additionally, you could combine Ho'oponopono with breathing exercises to enhance relaxation.

By incorporating these practical exercises into your daily life, you create a dynamic and responsive Ho'oponopono practice. Developing a personalised routine and adapting techniques to fit changing needs ensures that you remain engaged with the practice and continue to benefit from its transformative power.

Points to Remember:

- **Create a Special Space**: Set up a quiet, comfortable spot at home where you can focus on your Ho'oponopono practice.
- **Build Daily Habits**: Use simple daily routines with phrases like "I'm sorry," "Please forgive me," "Thank you," and "I love you" to make the practice a regular part of your life.
- **Go Deeper**: Once you're comfortable, try longer meditations or combine Ho'oponopono with other practices like yoga or journaling to enhance your experience.
- **Make It Yours**: Customise your practice to fit your daily schedule and personal goals. Adjust as needed to keep it effective and meaningful.
- **Stay Flexible**: Be open to changing and adapting your practice as your life and needs evolve.

Chapter 9

The Journey Continues

"The journey of a thousand miles begins with a single step."

– Lao Tzu

The journey of Ho'oponopono is not a destination but an ongoing journey that offers endless opportunities for healing, growth, and personal transformation. As we conclude this guide, it's essential to recognise that Ho'oponopono is a lifelong practice that evolves and deepens with time and dedication. Ho'oponopono is a profound and dynamic practice rooted in Hawaiian tradition, designed to foster inner peace, reconciliation, and personal development. The essence of this practice lies in its continuous, cyclical nature. Unlike many approaches that might have a clear endpoint or final goal, Ho'oponopono is about the ongoing journey of self-discovery and healing.

1. Lifelong Practice

Ho'oponopono is not a destination but a path we walk throughout life. Ho'oponopono embodies the idea that personal growth and healing are ongoing processes rather than final goals. It is a continuous journey that invites us to engage with our inner world and external relationships in a meaningful way. By embracing Ho'oponopono as a lifelong practice, we acknowledge that the principles of this tradition can guide us through various stages of life, helping us navigate challenges and cultivate a deeper sense of peace and fulfilment.

A. Embracing Change:

a. **Continuous Learning and Adaptation:** Personal growth is naturally dynamic. As we move through different phases of life, we encounter new experiences, challenges, and insights. Ho'oponopono encourages us to view these changes as opportunities for further learning and adaptation. By remaining open to the evolving nature of our journey, we can continuously refine our practice and integrate new understanding.

b. Navigating Life's Transitions: Whether facing personal, professional, or relational transitions, Ho'oponopono provides a foundation for addressing and processing these changes. The principles of forgiveness, gratitude, and love remain relevant as we adapt to new circumstances, helping us maintain balance and clarity.

B. Daily Commitment:

a. **Integrating Practice into Everyday Life:** For Ho'oponopono to be truly transformative, it must become a natural and consistent part of our daily routine. This daily commitment involves incorporating the practice into various aspects of life, from handling everyday stresses to deepening our connections with others.

b. **Creating Rituals:** Establishing regular rituals, such as morning affirmations, meditative moments, or reflective journaling, helps reinforce the principles of Ho'oponopono. These practices create a structured approach to maintaining focus and commitment, ensuring that the practice remains a central part of your life.

c. **Consistency Over Perfection:** It is important to approach your practice with a mindset of consistency rather than perfection. Daily commitment does not mean you have to practice perfectly every day but rather that you stay engaged with the process. Flexibility and compassion towards yourself are key in maintaining a sustainable practice.

Practical Steps to Embrace Lifelong Practice:

a) Set Intentions: Define what you hope to achieve with your Ho'oponopono practice and how you want it to impact your life. These intentions will guide your approach and keep you motivated.

1. **Establish a Routine:** Develop a daily or weekly routine that includes Ho'oponopono practices. This could involve setting aside specific times for meditation, affirmations, or reflection.
2. **Adapt and Evolve:** Be prepared to adapt your practice as your life circumstances change. Adjust your routines, techniques, and focus areas to stay aligned with your current needs and goals.
3. **Reflect and Journal:** Regularly reflect on your experiences and insights gained from your practice. Keeping a journal can help track progress, understand patterns, and deepen your self-awareness.
4. **Seek Support:** Engage with a community or find resources that support your practice. Sharing experiences and learning from others can enhance your understanding and commitment.

5. **Celebrate Growth:** Acknowledge and celebrate the positive changes and growth you experience through your practice. Recognising your progress reinforces the value of your commitment and encourages continued effort.

By viewing Ho'oponopono as a lifelong path, you embrace the continuous nature of personal development and healing. This perspective helps you integrate the practice into your daily life, navigate life's changes with resilience, and cultivate a sustained connection with the transformative principles of Ho'oponopono.

2. Ongoing Transformation

The journey with Ho'oponopono is marked by continuous personal transformation. As you engage with its principles and practices, you progressively uncover deeper layers of understanding about yourself and your interactions with the world. This ongoing transformation is a core aspect of the practice, reflecting its capacity to facilitate profound and lasting change in your life.

A. Celebrating Progress:

a. **Recognising Achievements:** As you incorporate Ho'oponopono into your life, it's important to take note of the progress you make. Whether it's improved emotional resilience, enhanced relationships, or a deeper sense of inner peace, acknowledging these changes reinforces the value of your practice.

b. **Marking Milestones:** Celebrate key moments or milestones in your journey. These might include achieving a personal goal, overcoming a challenge, or experiencing a breakthrough in understanding. Celebrating these achievements fosters a positive mindset and motivates you to continue your practice.

c. **Gratitude and Reflection:** Take time to express gratitude for the growth and insights gained through your practice. Reflect on how these changes have impacted your life and the lives of those around you. This reflection enhances your appreciation of the practice and its benefits.

Practical Steps for Celebrating Progress:

Keep a journal of your experiences and accomplishments related to Ho'oponopono. Create rituals or activities to celebrate milestones, such as a special meditation session or a day of reflection. Share your progress with a supportive community or loved ones to reinforce your achievements.

B. Facing Challenges:

a. **Viewing Obstacles as Growth Opportunities:** Challenges and obstacles are an inevitable part of life and practice. Ho'oponopono encourages you to view these difficulties as opportunities for further growth and learning. Each challenge provides a chance to apply the principles of forgiveness, gratitude, and love in new ways.

b. **Learning from Difficulties:** When faced with challenges, use Ho'oponopono to explore underlying issues and patterns. This approach helps you gain deeper insights into your reactions and behaviours, fostering personal development.

c. **Resilience and Adaptation:** Embrace a mindset of resilience and adaptability. By approaching obstacles with openness and curiosity, you can navigate difficulties more effectively and integrate the lessons learned into your practice.

Practical Steps for Facing Challenges:

When encountering a challenge, use the Ho'oponopono phrases to address the situation. For example, apply "I'm sorry," "Please forgive me," "Thank you," and "I love you" to the obstacle or your response to it. Reflect on the lessons or insights gained from the challenge. Consider how these experiences can contribute to your ongoing growth and transformation. Seek support or guidance from others who have navigated similar challenges.

Learning from their experiences can provide valuable perspectives and strategies.

Examples:

Celebrating Progress: After consistently practising Ho'oponopono for a few months, you may notice a greater sense of inner peace and improved communication in your relationships. Celebrate this progress by dedicating a day to reflection and gratitude, acknowledging how the practice has positively impacted your life.

Facing Challenges: Suppose you encounter a significant conflict at work. Instead of viewing it as a setback, use Ho'oponopono to address any underlying issues and apply the principles to facilitate resolution. Reflect on what this challenge reveals about your patterns and growth areas, and use this understanding to enhance your practice.

By embracing the ongoing transformation that comes with Ho'oponopono, you deepen your engagement with the practice and continue to evolve in meaningful ways. Celebrating progress and facing challenges with a positive and reflective mindset enriches your journey, allowing you to experience the full potential of Ho'oponopono's transformative power.

Practical Exercises

To ensure that Ho'oponopono remains a meaningful and integral part of your life, developing effective strategies for maintaining a lifelong practice is essential. This involves creating a long-term action plan and regularly setting and updating personal intentions. These practical exercises help sustain your commitment, adapt to changes, and continually align your practice with your personal growth.

a) Long-term Action Plan:

i. **Creating a Roadmap:** Develop a comprehensive plan that outlines how you will integrate Ho'oponopono into your life over the long term. This plan should include specific goals, milestones, and strategies to help you stay on track with your practice.

ii. **Identifying Goals:** Define clear, long-term objectives for your Ho'oponopono practice. These might include deepening your understanding of the principles, improving specific areas of your life, or achieving greater emotional resilience.

iii. **Establishing Milestones:** Break down your long-term goals into smaller, achievable milestones. For example, if your goal is to enhance personal growth, set milestones such as completing a series of advanced meditations or participating in a Ho'oponopono workshop.

iv. **Planning Regular Reviews:** Schedule regular check-ins to evaluate your progress and make adjustments to your action plan as needed. These reviews help you stay focused and address any challenges or changes in your practice.

Practical Steps for Developing a Long-term Action Plan:

a. **Write Down Your Goals:** Document your long-term goals and milestones in a dedicated journal or planner. This serves as a reference and reminder of your objectives.

b. **Create a Timeline:** Develop a timeline for achieving your milestones and goals. Include dates for regular reviews to assess your progress.

c. **Adjust as Needed:** Be flexible and willing to adjust your action plan based on your experiences and evolving needs. Update your plan to reflect any new insights or changes in your life.

Example: If your long-term goal is to enhance inner peace through Ho'oponopono, your action plan might include daily practice, monthly reflections, attending a retreat annually, and periodically revisiting and revising your practice based on your evolving needs and experiences.

b) Setting Intentions:

a. **Regularly Reviewing Goals:** Periodically review and reassess your personal goals related to Ho'oponopono. This helps ensure that your practice remains aligned with your current needs and aspirations.

b. **Updating Intentions:** Adjust your goals and intentions as your understanding and practice of Ho'oponopono evolves. This might involve setting new objectives, refining existing ones, or shifting focus based on your progress and experiences.

c. **Aligning with Practice:** Ensure that your intentions are in harmony with the core principles of Ho'oponopono. This alignment helps maintain the integrity and effectiveness of your practice.

Practical Steps for Setting and Updating Intentions:

a. **Reflect on Your Journey:** Take time to reflect on your progress and experiences with Ho'oponopono. Consider what has worked well and what areas may need further attention.

b. **Write Down New Intentions:** Update your goals and intentions in your journal or planner. Clearly articulate how these new or refined intentions align with your ongoing practice.

c. **Incorporate into Practice:** Integrate your updated intentions into your daily practice. For example, if your new goal is to improve communication skills, incorporate specific affirmations or visualisations related to this objective.

Example: If you initially focused on self-forgiveness and now wish to enhance your relationships, update your intentions to include practices that address interpersonal dynamics. Adjust your action plan to include new exercises, such as visualisation for improving communication and incorporating Ho'oponopono principles into relationship interactions.

By developing a long-term action plan and regularly setting and updating intentions, you create a structured and adaptable framework for maintaining a lifelong Ho'oponopono practice. These practical exercises ensure that your journey with Ho'oponopono remains dynamic, relevant, and aligned with your personal growth and evolving needs.

Conclusion

In conclusion, "The Alchemy of Peace" is an invitation to embark on a transformative journey towards inner peace and self discovery through the timeless principles of Ho'oponopono. The book highlights that true peace is not a final destination but a continuous process of personal and emotional growth, much like turning base materials into gold. By integrating practices like forgiveness, gratitude, and self-love into daily life, you learn to heal past wounds, release emotional burdens, and create deeper connections with yourself and others.

Through practical exercises, reflective journaling, and daily affirmations, "The Alchemy of Peace" offers a roadmap to transform negative emotions into opportunities for growth, fostering a more compassionate and fulfilling life. Whether you are new to Ho'oponopono or deepening your practice, this book serves as a guide to help you embrace the alchemical power of self-healing and emotional transformation.

The beauty of this journey is in its simplicity—saying sorry, forgiving, expressing gratitude and extending unconditional love have the profound ability to create lasting peace and balance. As you explore the chapters, you will find yourself equipped with tools and techniques to continue evolving, adapting, and nurturing your inner peace, ensuring it flourishes amidst life's challenges. Ultimately, "The Alchemy of Peace" reminds us that the journey towards inner peace is ongoing, and by embracing the principles of Ho'oponopono, we can cultivate a life filled with harmony, resilience, and love.

Tips and Tricks for Practising Ho'oponopono

To help you seamlessly integrate Ho'oponopono into your daily life and make it a transformative part of your journey, here are some practical tips and tricks:

1. Start Simple

Tip: Begin with the basics. The core phrases of Ho'oponopono are "I'm sorry," "Please forgive me," "Thank you," and "I love you." Use these phrases to address any issue or feeling of discomfort.

Trick: Write these phrases on sticky notes and place them in visible areas (e.g., your mirror, desk) as gentle reminders throughout your day.

2. Establish a Routine.

Tip: Incorporate Ho'oponopono into your daily routine. Dedicate specific times each day to practice, such as in the morning or before bed.

Trick: Set a daily alarm or reminder on your phone to practice Ho'oponopono. Consistency helps make the practice a natural part of your life.

3. Create a Ritual

Tip: Develop a personal ritual that resonates with you. This could include meditation, journaling, or reflection while repeating the Ho'oponopono phrases.

Trick: Combine Ho'oponopono with another calming activity you enjoy, such as sipping tea or taking a walk. Associating it with a positive experience can enhance its effectiveness.

4. Use Visualisations

Tip: Visualise the process of healing and resolution. Picture yourself and others involved in a peaceful and loving interaction as you repeat the Ho'oponopono phrases.

Trick: Create a vision board with images and words that represent peace and healing. Use it as a focus during your practice.

5. Be Patient and Compassionate.

Tip: Understand that Ho'oponopono is a process, not an instant fix. Be patient with yourself and the outcomes.

Trick: Keep a journal to document your thoughts and feelings before and after practising Ho'oponopono. Reflecting on your progress can help you see the gradual changes.

6. Apply to Relationships

Tip: Use Ho'oponopono to address conflicts or issues in your relationships. Apply the practice to yourself and others to foster forgiveness and understanding.

Trick: Send a silent prayer or intention of Ho'oponopono to people you find challenging. Visualise healing and resolution happening between you.

7. Practice Gratitude.

Tip: Integrate gratitude into your Ho'oponopono practice by acknowledging and appreciating the lessons and growth that come from your experiences.

Trick: Keep a gratitude journal where you write down things you're thankful for each day. Include the positive changes you observe from practising Ho'oponopono.

8. Seek Support

Tip: Connect with others who practise Ho'oponopono to share experiences and gain insights. Being part of a community can provide encouragement and guidance.

Trick: Join online forums, local groups, or workshops dedicated to Ho'oponopono. Engaging with a community can enhance your practice and provide additional resources.

9. Embrace Flexibility.

Tip: Be open to adapting your practice as your needs and circumstances evolve. Ho'oponopono can be personalised to fit different aspects of your life.

Trick: Experiment with different techniques and approaches within Ho'oponopono. Find what resonates most with you and make adjustments as needed.

10. Celebrate Progress.

Tip: Recognise and celebrate the positive changes and growth that come from practising Ho'oponopono. Acknowledging your progress reinforces your commitment.

Trick: Create a ritual for celebrating milestones, such as treating yourself to something special or reflecting on your achievements in a dedicated space.

By incorporating these tips and tricks, you can make Ho'oponopono a natural and impactful part of your daily life. Remember, the key is consistency, openness, and a willingness to embrace the transformative journey.

www.ingramcontent.com/pod-product-compliance
Lightning Source LLC
LaVergne TN
LVHW091051150826
845673LV00002B/537

* 9 7 9 8 8 9 7 2 4 0 7 0 8 *